William W. Oliver,
Dec. 27, 1995



# WHY WE SHOULD ABOLISH THE INCOME TAX:

## A Guide to the Principal Proposals

by

William W. Oliver

**Cross Cultural Publications, Inc.**

*CrossRoads Books*

CROSS CULTURAL PUBLICATIONS, INC.
CROSS ROADS BOOKS

Published by **CROSS CULTURAL PUBLICATIONS, INC.**
**CROSS ROADS BOOKS**
Post Office Box 506
Notre Dame, Indiana, 46556, U.S.A.
Phone: (219) 273-6526, 1-800-561-6526
FAX: (219) 273-5973


ISBN: 0-940121-33-6
Library of Congress Catalog Card Number: 95-71215

**DEDICATION**

**I dedicate this book to my wife**

**Mary Morgan Oliver**

**I could not have married a more wonderful person.**

**Without her I would not have two fine children,**

**Barbara Ann Oliver**

**and**

**William Morgan Oliver**

**I am proud of them both.**

## ACKNOWLEDGMENTS

Dean Alfred Aman of the School of Law, Indiana University, Bloomington, made funds available for me to hire law students as research assistants. Three students—now lawyers—Joan Tupin-Crites, Carol Adinamis, and Cathy Prohofsky, assisted with the research for this book. All three did superb work. We are gaining by having more women in the legal profession. I recommend all three to anyone in search of reliable, capable legal counsel, especially in the tax area. Joan is in Columbus, Indiana; Carol practices in Indianapolis; and Cathy works for Chief Counsel of Internal Revenue in Washington, D.C.

Three women were my secretaries during the time the book was underway: Rachel Myers, Krystie Herndon, and Mary Jo Dragojlovic. All were cheerful, prompt and careful in their work. My wife and I consider Rachel (who worked for me longer than the other two) a friend of the family.

Dale Swihart, a former student of mine and Professor of Law and Director of the Graduate Tax Program at Washington University, St. Louis, MO., read the manuscript and made valuable suggestions. While I was a visiting professor there in the summer of 1982 I learned that he was highly respected by the staff, faculty, and students. He is a thoroughly decent person.

Henry Geller, a classmate of mine in law school, and a nationally known and admired person in communications law, also read the bulk of the manuscript. He encouraged me by expressing his opinion that I had made a case for abolition of the income tax. He also suggested that I omit the language about vote buying with public funds. Despite my admiration for his intelligence and judgment, I did not delete that language. My opinion is that vote buying with public funds is the essence of modern politics and the primary cause for the growth of federal spending, deficits and the national debt.

The copy editor for Cross Cultural Publications, Joan Marie Laflamme, improved the language and I thank her.

## PREFACE

When I graduated from Northwestern Law School in 1949, I decided that federal taxation was a coming field and that specialization was becoming increasingly necessary in the practice of law. My savings from my service in the Army Air Corps in World War II were nearly gone, and my right to tuition and a monthly allowance under the G.I. Bill of Rights were nearing an end.

Rather than trying to go to a graduate program in tax, such as the excellent one at New York University School of Law, I sought and obtained employment as a trial attorney with Chief Counsel's Office in the Bureau of Internal Revenue (now the Internal Revenue Service). At the end of three years, based upon a recommendation from the Northwestern Law School, I received a two-year appointment as a law clerk to Chief Justice Fred M. Vinson of the United States Supreme Court. He died of a heart attack near the end of my first year with him. Chief Justice Earl Warren replaced him and kept Justice Vinson's law clerks. I served him one year as his head law clerk.

At that point my credentials would point to practice as a tax lawyer in a large firm in a large city. However, I decided during a traffic jam on the Fourteenth Street bridge (between Virginia and Washington, D.C.) that I did not want to live in a large city and would seek a position as a tax professor at a law school in a smaller city. I joined the faculty at the Indiana University School of Law at Bloomington, Indiana, in September 1954 and retired there on December 31, 1991.

When I left my position as a trial attorney with Internal Revenue, I realized that it could be wrong at times, but believed it general to be correct in the positions it took. My confidence in the Service was shaken by my experience in trying to obtain a court precedent that the research expenses of professors were deductible under the federal income tax laws. The shameful conduct of Internal revenue in that effort is related in Chapter 2 of this book.

That experience led me to wonder just what really was the vast phenomenon brought into existence by the federal income tax law. The rules of Indiana University permit a law faculty member to devote up to twenty percent of his time to practice and consultation, and I took advantage of that.

Working with lawyers and CPAs helped me keep in touch with reality and avoid the fanaticism that often comes from talking only with academicians (especially the "politically correct"). When at tax institutes, alumni meetings, and in other contacts with tax attorneys and CPAs, I made it a practice to ask about how the income tax was working. Much of what I write in this book reflects what I learned from countless conversations. There was a consistency in what I heard. In the past ten years or so there has emerged a growing literature about the problems with the income tax and the Internal Revenue Service. Some of that literature is quoted and discussed in chapter 1 to show that my position that the Income Tax should be abolished is similar to that of may others familiar with the administration of that tax.

The small businesses of Indiana elected me as a delegate to all three White House Conferences on Small Business (1980, 1986, and 1995). Many meetings at the state level preceded the meetings in Washington, D.C. Much antagonism toward the income tax and the IRS was expressed in those meetings. I was accepted once the small businessmen realized that I too saw much wrong with the income tax system.

# PREFACE

Much writing about the income tax is difficult for laymen to understand. Myriad details have to be incorporated in order to be 100 percent accurate. I have simplified in an effort to make this book readable by and useful to ordinary citizens. I, therefore, warn tax experts that many details are missing.

Discussion about what to do regarding the income tax mess is on-going. Doubtless there will be developments in the future which are, of necessity, not reflected in the book as it is being readied for the printer.

# TABLE OF CONTENTS

# 1
# INTRODUCTION

A history teacher asked the class, "What caused the American Revolution?" A little girl answered, "Taxation." A little boy raised his hand, and the teacher said, "Yes, Tommy." He asked, "Why do the history books say we won?"

The problems with the federal income tax are vast. During my forty-six years in dealing with federal taxation, the income tax has become worse and worse. Abolishing it is the solution.

The state legislators who ratified the income tax amendment to the Constitution believed that it was a simple and fair tax. Eighty years of experience have proved they were mistaken.

As the income tax has evolved, it has become so complicated that only highly intelligent people with years of experience can handle much of it; no one can understand it all, for much of it is virtually incomprehensible. Only the rare Congressman will understand much of it; full-time candidates for re-election simply do not have the time to learn much about such a difficult subject.

Staff members to the Joint Committee on Internal Revenue, as well as the policy makers in the Treasury Department, lack experience in the day-to-day administration of the income tax. Complexity is added on top of existing complexity. Franklin said that death and taxes are always with us, but at least death doesn't get worse each time Congress meets.Complying with the income tax legislation imposes a costly burden on the American people, over and above the income tax paid. James L. Payne in ***Costly Returns*** concluded that the compliance costs, plus other direct and indirect costs, are $0.65 for every dollar in revenue received by the federal government. Thus tax lawyers and tax accountants refer to new income tax legislation as the "Full

Employment Act for Lawyers and Accountants." But what a shaft for the American people!

The income tax is full of discriminations. There is massive cheating. Inflation results in taxing as income amounts which are not really income. This is especially true of capital gains after a holding period of many years. Inflation causes actual losses to many people, and they cannot deduct these on their income tax returns.

The complexity of the income tax causes numerous errors, both by IRS personnel and others. As a practical matter, complexity means the IRS cannot achieve fair administration; that is, treat similar situations the same from agent to agent and across the country.

Many people do not experience the vexation of the income tax. Those who have only income subject to withholding, who have few deductions, and who receive refunds are generally not troubled by the income tax. The income tax treats unfairly small businesses, self-employed persons, and persons with above-average incomes. The current system is a tyranny of the majority on these groups.

Jimmy Carter said, "The income tax is a disgrace to the human race." Below are quotations from some of the most respected names of persons who know the federal income tax well. Quotations from their work support Jimmy Carter's—and my opinion—of the federal income tax.

• **James S. Eustice**, (1989) "Complexity and Practitioners" 45 ***Tax Law*** R.7.

> p. 8 "I'm gradually coming to believe that matters are in danger of getting out of control."
> p. 11 "There are many reasons why this com plexity crisis has developed."
> p. 13 "Congress, of course, being the fountain head of legislation, is perforce the major 'villain' in the complexity scenario. They started it all; they wrote it."

> p. 15 "Thus, it is not surprising that the vast outpouring of tax law cases in certain areas tends eventually to become overwhelming to the point of near meaninglessness."
> Fn. 22 "The Supreme Court is also a loose cannon on a rolling deck."

James S. Eustice is the Gerald L. Wallace Professor of Law, New York University. While no one can be on top of all the complexities of the income tax, he and Boris L. Bittker, Sterling Professor Emeritus of Law, Yale University, probably come as close as possible.

• **Joseph Isenbergh**, (1989), in his article "The End of Income Taxation" appearing at 45 ***Tax Law R***. 283 says:

> p. 284 "In short, capital formation in the U.S. is weaker than it would be with a different tax system."
> p. 298 "The main suppliers of capital are for eign, and operate outside the U.S. income tax system and are untaxed by it."
> p. 302 "What followed the 1986 Act was a large tax driven increase in the level of debt in U.S. corporations."
> p. 314 "There are signs that the administration of the income tax is sagging badly, if not breaking down altogether."
> p. 315 "To increase public revenues by adding additional IRS auditors, while perhaps inevi table if we are to muddle through with the present tax system, is itself a cause of lower real GNP."
> p.360 "The basic failure of our income tax is far more apparent today than it was in the mid 1970s, despite its then having been proclaimed by James Earl Carter a 'disgrace to the human race'."
> p. 361 "What is at stake in the unfolding politi cal contest over taxation is how consumers and suppliers of capital will fare vis-a-vis each

> other as the United States lurches toward the millennium. It is not yet 1789 (when one of the world's great economic powers came apart after losing its hold on its fiscal destiny), but it is later than you think."

Isenbergh is a Professor of Law at the University of Chicago.

•**Jennie L Statis**, (Sept.1989) who was the Director of Tax Policy and Administration, General Accounting Office, in her article "Is the IRS Underfunded?" ***Journal of Accountancy*** indicates that the percentage of audits is low (p. 77). She sees a need for "a credible audit potential" to discourage taxpayers from "playing the audit lottery" (taking a position on an income tax return which is questionable, because the chance of the return being audited is low and even if the return is audited, the item may be overlooked by the auditor).

She also points to the need to upgrade the quality of IRS answers to taxpayers' telephone calls "because studies both by the G.A.O. and IRS found telephone assistors continued to answer about one third of test calls incorrectly" (p. 78).

• ***Journal of Accountancy***, News Column (March 1990,) p.16. In this report on a survey of one thousand C.P.A. tax practitioners we read:

> "[The IRS] suffers from communication problems and a lack of technical knowledge at its lower personnel levels," and budgetary constraints prevent adequate staff training" (quoting Donald H. Shaddon, A.I.C.P.A. Vice President Taxation).
>
> "Most significantly," the article continues, "the C.P.A.'s surveyed blamed Congress for the numerous, complex and constantly changing tax laws that have created a tax system that is extremely difficult for the IRS to effectively and consistently administer."
>
> The News Column continued saying that "IRS personnnel are frequently inexperienced and lack basic accounting and tax skills." This is attributed by the

CPAs surveyed to the relatively low pay scale at the IRS. Over 90 percent rated appeals officers excellent or good.

• "**Fred Goldberg** and His Mission Improbable, ***Business Week*** (March 26, 1990),

> "The big challenge of the coming decade is finding ways to make the tax system workable for the American public" (p. 80).

The clear implication in Goldberg's statement (Goldberg was then Commissioner of Internal Revenue) is that the tax system is presently unworkable.

• **David F. Bradford**, (1986) ***Untangling theIncome Tax,*** Harvard Univesity Press,

> "A law that can be understood, if at all, by only a tiny priesthood of lawyers and accoun tants is naturally subject to popular suspicion. By undermining popular support, complex-ity erodes the self assessment on which eco nomical compliance depends" (p. 266).

Professor Bradford is at Princeton University.

• **Charles McLure, Jr.**, in his article, The Budget Process and Tax Simplification/Complication, appearing in 45 ***Tax Law* R.**25, 69 (1989) notes that Congress has enacted many new penalties, then says:

> "But it appears that in the process of making penalties and interest rules tighter, not enough attention has been devoted to rationalizing penalties. Thus layer upon layer of penalties are piled upon each other, producing a system that is complicated as well as arguably un fair."

• **David Burnham**, ***A Law Unto Itself—Power Politics and the IRS,*** also portrays a tax system in trouble. The book is well-written, clearly reflecting extensive research.

My difference with Burnham is one of emphasis, for there is material in his book relevant to my two main theses: first, Congress, not the IRS, is the major problem; and second, there is a constant increase in complexity, created primarily by Congress, which is making the federal income tax increasingly unworkable.

Congress doesn't know what it is doing with the income tax. Members know one or two principal items as reported by the news media. If there is some "fund-raising" provision, repaying influential constituents or contributors, a member is aware of that provision. But understanding the overall operation of the system is beyond almost all members, although through the years there have been some members who became tax experts. Fred M. Vinson, Wilbur Mills and Barber Conable, are three such tax experts.

The national news media lack the expertise to explain complex tax issues, and the general public is unable to follow the discussion of most tax issues. Thus there is the opportunity for a member to bury a provision in the tax law that aids a few people, with little risk of exposure. (Why do you think members of the Ways and Means Committee and the Senate Finance Committee receive "contributions" in excess of the average amounts received by other members of Congress?)

• **James L. Payne**, ***Costly Returns. The Burdens of the U.S. Tax System,*** (San Francisco, ICS Press, 1993) is an important book that should be widely read. Payne does a thorough job of analyzing the total monetary costs of the federal tax system for the year 1985 (almost all of this cost falls on the private sector, not the federal government). The total cost for 1985 was $362.9 billion, or just over 65 percent of the available revenue collected that year. Payne acknowledged that a study of the 1983 tax year by Arthur D. Little, commissioned by the Internal Revenue Service as required by the 1980 Paperwork Reduction Act, developed methodologies used by him in his study.

One cost that Payne appears not to have put into dollars is the cost to other persons resulting from audits of another taxpayer. It is difficult to put a dollar figure on this, but it is a significant cost, especially to banks, savings and loan associations, insurance companies and so on.. Wholesalers, realtors, insurance agents, suppliers of various items, building contractors, and so forth, can be compelled to open their records to and be interviewed by Service auditors. If the other person party is asked to reproduce portions of his or her records pertaining to another taxpayer being audited (which uses up the time of that person and employees), he or she may comply out of the fear that many persons have of the Internal Revenue Service. Of course, if these people have major tax items on which they played the "audit lottery," they are in a dilemma when asked to open their records. If they comply, the agent may stumble across such items. If they do not comply, the agent may become suspicious and order a full audit on them.

These consequential costs of the federal income tax are economically unproductive. Another revenue scheme could be simpler and less costly. Eliminating the income tax would be a boon to our economy. Further, many of those working in the tax field are intelligent and able people who could make valuable contributions to society in other roles. Funds no longer wasted by businesses on complying with or working to avoid the income tax could give a strong impetus to the economy.

Many small businesses do, of course, offset some and perhaps all the cost of the income tax by tax avoidance and even tax evasion. But do we do ourselves a service by a tax system with a strong inducement for dishonesty?

Let us for the time being accept Payne's estimate that the income tax imposes cost on the private sector equal to 65 percent of the revenue it raises. Because compliance costs are minimal for many tax payers—those with all income subject to withholding and who use the standard deduction—the cost to the other taxpayers must be much greater. In order for the average to reach

65 percent, the group with more complicated tax returns must actually incur costs far above 65 percent of the tax they pay. Small businesses on the average probably carry a heavier burden, paying far more than 65 percent in compliance costs. Larger businesses typically have resources available to cope more successfully with the income tax than do small businesses.

As a remedy for this astounding consequential cost from the federal income tax, Payne proposes that the federal government compensate taxpayers for their costs resulting from the federal tax system. While that would be just, I find it unlikely that Congress would give up substantial public funds to productive citizens (taxpayers) rather than using those public funds to buy the votes of "buyable" citizens, many of whom are unproductive and not taxpayers. The proper remedy is to abolish the federal income tax.

• Another recent book relevant to the federal income tax is **Charles Adams**'s, ***For Good and Evil: The Impact of Taxes on the Course of Civilization,*** (Lanham, MD. Madison Books. 1993). The dedication to his book reads,

> To our children in the twenty-first century—with the hope that they may be creative and develop a tax system devoid of the evils that permeate the system under which we now live.

Charles Adams holds a doctor of law degree from UCLA. He has spent most of his professional career in international taxation outside the United States. His scholarly interests have resulted in lecturing and writing both about the history of taxation and present-day tax systems.

Most of Adams's book is devoted to the history of taxation in various civilizations, and how bad tax systems have led to the decline of those civilizations. I understand his title ***For Good and Evil*** to imply that the revenue from taxes can be used to accomplish good, but that tax systems can also be evil and harmful. He clearly thinks the present U.S. tax system, which is primarily the income tax, is in the evil category. Adams refers to "America's insanely complex income tax" (p. 471).

Just as with Burnham's book, my difference with Adams is one of emphasis. I am more tolerant of Internal Revenue Service people than he; and I see them as simply trying to do their job enforcing a law. Congress does not have the knowledge to deal with the income tax area. Committee staff members and Treasury Department personnel really determine income tax policy. Yet, these people are out of touch with the reality of the income tax across the United States. They are particularly unaware of what the income tax does to small businesses and self-employed persons.

• Excerpts from remarks by **Erwin N. Griswold** before the Annual Meeting of the American College of Tax Counsel, San Diego, California, February 5, 1993:

> It is a great honor to be invited to speak before this group—and, indeed, to have a lectureship established in my name. I am grateful to those of you who have brought this about, and hope that this may result in a series of lectures which will help to make our tax system more understandable and workable.
>
> I have one further point, which is a major one. It can be put concisely: the present tax law has spun out complications to the extent that it is truly monstrous. In my view, something must be done about it.
>
> The net result, in my view, is that our present tax system, which worked very well during the first third of this century, and struggled along during the second third of the century, has now come to the place where it is simply monstrous. We would never accept it if it had not just crept up on us.

Erwin Griswold was Dean of the Harvard Law School from 1946 to 1967 and Solicitor General of the U.S. from 1967 to 1973.

Dean Griswold speaks of the monstrous code having "just crept up on us." For me the 1982 TEFRA was the straw of complexity that broke the camel's back. Howard Baker was majority leader in the Senate at that time, and Bob Dole was chairman of the Senate Finance Committee. Griswold's speech appears at 11 ***American Journal of Tax Policy*** p. 1.

In fact, the United States has taxation without representation. Perhaps it's time for a second American Revolution. It need not be violent. All that is needed is to vote against every Congressman who voted for the 1993 Clinton tax bill. It carried so narrowly that a switch of only one vote in either the House or the Senate would have prevented its passage. (Chapter 16 discusses some of the objectionable provisions in that bill.)

# 2
# THE CURRENT SCENE

## In the Field

The relationship between the IRS personnel in the field and taxpayers and their representatives is largely adversarial, with antagonism widespread. Morale of Service personnel is poor. Their friendships and socializing are primarily with other IRS employees and their families. One former IRS employee (married to antoher IRS employee) told me that when meeting other persons they would not reveal their IRS employment, saying only that they worked for the government. The amount of suffering resulting from the income tax has been enormous, and has lessened the favorable attitudes of citizens toward their government.

Cheating and playing the "audit lottery" are widespread among taxpayers. At a luncheon recently, the Indiana District Director (chief IRS officer in Indiana) reminded me that several million dependent children "disappeared" when income tax returns were changed to call for the social security numbers of dependent children.

Starting about twenty years ago, many individuals became "tax protesters." The protesters were mostly blue-collar or lived in rural areas. Protesters argued that the income tax was invalid on such grounds as that the income tax amendment (16th) was not properly ratified by the states or that the currency is invalid because the gold standard has been abandoned. Tax practitioners did not take their arguments seriously. While no reliable estimate can be made of their numbers, they were numerous (possibly hundreds of thousands, maybe as many as a few million) and bitterly resented by IRS personnel. Some of the recruits and resources for the militia and the patriot movements may have come from these protesters and other persons who believe they have been treated wrongly by the IRS. Abolishing the income tax may help reverse the growing sense of alienation from the federal government which many feel.

Congress enacted new penalties aimed at the protestors, and the courts summarily rejected the protest arguments and routinely imposed the penalties. To reject the protesters as an insignificant fringe has been a mistake; instead, the tax protest movement is just one of the symptoms showing us that the income tax and the Internal Revenue Service are widely despised. I do not believe, hoever, that the IRS alone is to blamc for the deplorable situation. Part of the problem is inherent in a net income tax, collected annually, and highly progressive. Congress through the years has heaped on complexities not germane to a net income tax, failed to take action to remove improper provisions from our Internal Revenue Code, and failed to understand the consequences of new provisions proposed by the Treasury Department or others. Abuses by taxpayers and tax practitioners have contributed to the development of complexities.

While the Service has extensive educational programs for its revenue agents, the current complexity of the income tax law is too much for most IRS employees. Many employees are recent accounting graduates who were in the lower part of their classes (pay is too low to hire from the top of the class).

There is massive cheating by taxpayers, and revenue agents have no magic looking-glass to identify honest taxpayers and honest tax practitioners. The burden of proof is on the taxpayer (called substantiation). This burden is sometimes applied so strictly that taxpayers feel guilty until they can prove their innocence.

A tax which produces as much anguish as the income tax does should be abolished and replaced by a simple (not complex) tax, such as a national retail sales tax. Those who deal in cash, thus cheating on the income tax, would pay the sales tax as consumers.

In 1949, when I was just out of law school, I became a trial attorney for the Internal Revenue Service. The appeals officers and trial attorneys, who were older and more experienced, told of the income tax becoming more adversarial during their careers. During my career the trend toward increased antagonism has continued, and the average ability of revenue agents has dropped primarily because pay is inadequate compared to the private sector.

Another sign that the income tax is in trouble is the huge number of people who are not filing income tax returns, between 7 million and 10 million according to the IRS. The amount of assessments—an assessment means to IRS personnel that a tax is owed and payable—that the IRS has been unable to collect now totals more than 100 billion dollars. It would be even larger if the considerable amounts were not being written off as uncollectible. Also, partial payments are frequently accepted as full payment under what is called an "offer-in-compromise." Those who owe should be aware of both offers-in-compromise and installment payments. Filing bankruptcy is an option if the IRS tax claim exceeds available assets.

## Appeals Office and District Counsel

There are appeals offices in the Service, and these offices work with the attorneys in the district counsel's office, which is part of the regional commissioner's office. The appeals officers and the attorneys, along with the people in the top echelons of the regional commissioner's office, are the best in the field (that is, away from the national IRS headquarters). Deficiencies (additional income tax liabilities) proposed by an auditing revenue agent can be appealed to this level and will be dealt with by well-informed and usually experienced persons. Their approach is professional and courteous.

These appeals officers have the authority to make compromises, taking into account the "hazards of litigation." At the end of the audit, revenue agents ask a taxpayer to sign a consent to an assessment of additional tax, perhaps even representing that the issue is cut and dried, even though it is an issue on which appeals officers would probably grant a concession of one-half or more. If the consent is signed, there will never be a thirty day letter giving notice of a proposed deficiency. That notice informs a taxpayer about the right to appeal within thirty days by filing a protest and having a hearing before an appeals officer. Failing to get that notice means the taxpayer is unlikely to meet with an appeals officer. In extreme cases, this is fraud by the revenue agent, but there are no provisions for penalties against or indictments of such revenue agents; this is in stark contrast to the vast array of penalties and criminal provisions that taxpayers face. Unfortunately, IRS agents and collection officers cannot be fired for such treatment of taxpayers.

Some accountants are reluctant to recommend bringing in an attorney experienced in tax litigation to take an appeal, perhaps fearing loss of the client to the attorney. Nonetheless, any taxpayer faced with a proposed deficiency of a significant amount should get advice from an attorney experienced in tax litigation. If there are two sides to a tax dispute the taxpayer should not sign a consent pushed by a revenue agent; rather, he or she should go to appeals. A taxpayer may agree to a compromise with an appeals officer simply to get the matter over with, even though experienced counsel advises that he or she would most likely win completely if the issue were litigated.

One problem sometimes encountered by taxpayers or their representatives is that the revenue agent or collection officer (and/or his supervisors in the district office) will "back-door" the appeals officer. IRS employees may pass information orally, such as "the taxpayer is lying," which they would not dare put in a written report furnished to the taxpayer. In litigation, an attorney who "back-doors" the judge is engaging in unethical conduct; the better judges will not tolerate oral conversations with counsel without the opposing attorney being present or at least informed.

Perhaps a similar rule should be applied to appeals officers, but appeals is in a difficult position, because from time to time appeals officers have to rely upon IRS audit personnel for verification of facts presented by taxpayers' representatives.

## Small Cases

Small cases are those in which the amounts involved are such that contesting the issue is too expensive. The cost of going to appeals or litigating in court makes paying the proposed deficiency the most cost-effective course of action. There is no way to determine assessments of deficiencies in income tax that would have been totally or partially eliminated if it had been feasible to utilize competent counsel and go to appeals. In short, the Service assesses and collects a huge amount each year erroneously. Although the amount in most individual cases is relatively small:, the total could be as much as forty billion dollars a year. This issue cannot be the study of scholarly research because IRS files for specific taxpayers are not a public record.

If the assessment is against a taxpayer with assets, the additional tax will soon be paid, although it may leave a disgruntled taxpayer inclined to cheat in the future to "get it back." When the assessment is against a transient or person with little or negative net worth, the assessment will probably be written off as uncollectible after the Service spends still more money trying to collect the tax.

## National Office

The national office of Internal Revenue is divided between the top levels, which change with administrations, and the permanent, civil-service bureaucrats. The top level people are mostly quality people, to some extent influenced by some ideological bias, depending upon the administration. The rest of the personnel in the national office varies from excellent (a sizeable minority) to mediocre, to those unconcerned or incapable of doing quality work. These last individuals relish their pay which, although below that of the professionals with whom they work on the outside, is above what they would receive in the private sector for comparable effort and results. Some of the Service's best people get hired away for higher compensation, which tends to reduce the average quality of the remaining personnel.

My experience in three matters involving the Rulings section of the National Office perhaps affects my judgment about the quality of the personnel in the National Office. Two of those cases are discussed in chapter 14. They relate to the deplorable record of Congress and the Service in the area of deferred charitable giving.

The third story is about the action of the Rulings section concerning the deductibility of the research expenses of college and university professors. In 1954, about the time I joined the Indiana University law faculty, one of its nationally known and highly respected professors was Ralph Fuchs. He went on leave for two years to Washington, D.C., to serve as executive secretary of the American Association of University Professors (AAUP). While in that position he experienced numerous complaints from professors about the I.R.S. denying deductions for expenses incurred in doing their research. He asked me if I would donate my services to help with this question, and I agreed to do so.

The problem had arisen because of theU.S. Tax Court decision in Cardozo, 17 T.C. 3 (1951). Cardozo was a professor of history and romance languages at Catholic University in Washington. He tried his own case, and lost it; if he had been represented by competent and determined counsel he probably would have won.

I obtained a transcript of Professor Cardozo's testimony before the Tax Court. On cross-examination, the Service's attorney got him to make ill-advised, inaccurate admissions, which tended to depict research by a university professor as being a hobby. That is not true; research is part of the job description, especially at the larger institutions. If there is no research, the professor may soon be an ex-professor. If there is quality research, there will be salary increases and perhaps a job with a more prestigious and wealthier institution at a higher salary level. Indeed, the research done by professors, particularly in the fields of the physical and biological sciences (including medicine), has been of enormous benefit to our country and the entire world.

In the first test case I brought on behalf of the AAUP, my premise was that the Service personnel, and the Tax Court judge in Cardozo, did not understand the role of research in higher education. So a petition to take the depositions of the dean of faculties at Northwestern University and the president of Princeton University was filed. The Service's attorney contacted me and asked why I wanted to take their depositions. I replied that they would enable the Tax Court to understand the facts about the role of research at colleges and universities. The Service attorney soon informed me that the case would be conceded. I argued that there should be a published Tax Court opinion to reflect the concession, but in vain; courts exist to resolve conflicts. Once the Service said "we were wrong, the professor owes no tax," there was no controversy. The Tax Court refused to issue a written opinion after hearing my oral argument that it should.

Since no opinion was issued by the Tax Court, there was no precedent to appear in the many sources of income tax law. I did two things: First, I went to the national Rulings office of the IRS and obtained an oral promise to issue a published ruling recognizing the deductibility of research expenses of professors. Second, I wrote an article in the ***AAUP Bulletin*** to alert professors to the fact that the Service attorneys would not defend in court the position that professors could not deduct research expenses.

But professors continued to complain to the national AAUP. New test cases were filed, and the Service attorneys conceded each case when they learned I was the taxpayer's attorney. But no precedent could be obtained. The Rulings section continued to respond to my numerous inquiries by claiming that a published ruling would soon be issued saying professors could deduct research expenses. How much was unjustly taken from professors during a four- or five-year period is unascertainable. The revenue agent, upon finding the Cardozo decision, would believe that following it was correct, and an accountant or attorney could not find any precedent to the contrary in the voluminous body of cases, rulings, regulations, laws and so forth.

I was more naive then than I now am about the capacity of the IRS to be wrongheaded. If I had it all to do over, I would, one, try to get my article published in some source indexed into the tax literature, such as ***Taxes Magazine***, ***Journal of Taxation***, or the ***Tax Law Review***. Also, I would complain to Congressmen and Congressional oversight committees concerned about IRS conduct. Since the IRS was patently wrong, I would issue press statements and tried to get on talk shows.

The beginning of the end of the research expenses controversy began when Professor Davis of Pomona College, on advice of counsel, paid the additional tax resulting from the IRS disallowing his deduction of research expenses, and then filed a suit for refund in a federal district court. He lost because the federal judge thought the decision in the Cardozo case (the only precedent) was correct. When I learned of the case, I contacted Davis's attorney and offered my services for free, (AAUP paid out-of-pocket expenses) to take an appeal to the Ninth Circuit. Once the taxpayer and his attorney accepted my offer, the IRS's successful evasion of a precedent recognizing the deductibility of research expenses of college and university professors was doomed. Even a reversal of the district court opinion by a concession would leave the precedent in the body of tax law, the goal for which we had been striving.

After I filed my brief with the Ninth Circuit in support of the reversal of the district court, the Tax Division of the Department of Justice informed Internal Revenue that it would neither file a reply brief nor defend its position in oral argument before the Ninth Circuit. The result was a published ruling, Rev. Rul. 63-275, which recognizes that research expenses of professors are deductible. This ruling is not as helpful to professors now as it was in 1963, because one of the devious ways in which Congress (often at the urging of Treasury and the national office of IRS) has raised taxes (without calling it an increase in taxes) has been to allow the deduction of expenses of employees who have miscellaneous itemized deductions only to the extent these exceed 2 percent of adjusted gross income.

Was this evasion by the IRS of a precedent recognizing the deductibility of research expenses of professors a happenstance, or was it a symptom of a serious defect in the quality ofmany lifetime civil service employees?

**Taxpayers and Withholding**

There is a fundamental distinction between taxpayers with only income subject to withholding and taxpayers with income not subject to withholding.Those with only income subject to withholding and who take the standard deduction ( do not itemize deductions) have no cause for controversy with the IRS. Indeed, because withholding levels are high enough that most receive a sizeable refund, they may be happy with the income tax system. On the other hand, taxpayers not subject to withholding have to manage their cash flow to pay income taxes to the IRS. They have to file annually and pay estimated income tax quarterly. The relationship between the Service and these taxpayers is often bitter and antagonistic. Taxpayers who itemize deductions in total amounts above those considered "acceptable" by the Service may be selected for audit. The audit may be unpleasant, if taxpayers do not have adequate records, such as cancelled checks or receipts, to support the amounts deducted. A written explanation attached to the return of such taxpayers may avoid an audit.

For instance, say a taxpayer receives an inheritance (which is not income, although there may be an inheritance tax), The taxpayer knows the deceased person had made a pledge to a charitable organization which was not yet fully paid at death. So, the taxpayer pays off the pledge, which amounts to more than half of the taxpayer's income. Such a relatively large deduction is the type of item likely to trigger an audit. A written explanation of the facts, including the amount of the inheritance and the docket number for the court probate proceeding, would probably prevent an audit.

A similar situation could involve life insurance death proceeds, which also are not income.

A person whose income is normally subject to withholding may regularly or temporarily have income on which there is no withholding. This may involve the person with an audit and a rude shock. Say there is a pipefitter, working for an employer who withholds the income tax. On his off-duty time, the pipefitter does plumbing work for homeowners. Of course there is no withholding on this work. Further, such income might not be reported by the pipefitter and never would be taxed. If a homeowner happened to be an IRS employee, there might be an audit, especially if that employee was unhappy with the cost or the quality of the work.

Assume that a skilled union worker for an employer who regularly withholds income tax, becomes unemployed. He has a chance for a temporary job with a small contractor at lower (non-union) pay, which after withholding would be less than his unemployment compensation. He agrees to work "off the books." He is paid in cash without withholding of income tax or social security taxes. He also continues to collect unemployment compensation. And he does not report the income on his tax return. Both that small contractor and the worker are taking a chance. They risk not only penalties for non-payment of taxes, but criminal charges. Such cheating is not an uncommon occurrence, even though it is rarely detected. A similar situation can occur involving illegal aliens who work "off the books."

In contrast to employed persons, there is a large group whose income tax liability is not satisfied fully by withholding. This group includes small businessmen, self-employed persons (including professional persons in partnerships), and persons with investment income only. Among these people there is widespread disgust with the income tax system and antagonism toward the IRS. They comprise only about 20 percent of the population and voters so it is unlikely that their political impact is sufficient to get the income tax abolished, however meritorious their arguments are.

There are at least three possible changes that would soon lead to sufficient political opposition to bring about the abolition of the income tax: One, end withholding and make it the obligation of each person to pay his or her income tax monthly, quarterly or annually. Second, lower the level of withholding sufficiently to oblige most employees to declare and pay estimated income tax quarterly. Third, enact a "truth in taxation" scheme, increasing withholding by 1/11 for January through November, and eliminating withholding in December. This would illustrate the true effect of the income tax.

The abolition of withholding would be a disaster. Many taxpayers would spend so much of their increased paychecks that they would not have enough funds to pay their income tax. Receipts of the federal government would drop significantly, and the resultant increase in the budget deficit might be enough to disturb capital markets, not only in the United States but worldwide.

The reduction of withholding amounts, so that few employees get refunds and most would have to pay some income tax, would soon result in enough political opposition to secure the abolition of the income tax. Don't forget that there already is a core of about 20 percent of the adult population who despise our current income tax and its administration.

Eliminating withholding in December would probably result in the abolition of the income tax before long. Many people adjust to their take-home pay as their pay; they only abstractly realize how much they are paying as income tax to the federal government. Getting wage or salary checks in December unreduced by withholding of federal taxes would stimulate Christmas sales and the enjoyment of the Christmas season. It also would be a realistic lesson that federal spending lowers the living standards of most people, although government spending does raise the living standards of the welfare class, a very large component of the "grow-the-government "party. If voters really understood this, many would vote against candidates who want to "grow" the federal government.

**Audit Lottery**

The percentage of returns audited (the audit rate) has tbeen decreasing in recent years, although it may be rising again now. The decrease is partially a result of the increasing complexity and length of the Internal Revenue Code. Congressional action leads to new schedules, new forms, and lengthened old forms. It takes longer to prepare returns. although the use of computers can help to reduce the time needed. The more complicated returns increase the time needed for each audit. The longer audits take, the fewer audits can be done. Tax practitioners, as well as business and investment taxpayers, are aware of this. The low audit rate encourages taxpayers to take a chance that their return will not be audited. Therefore, taxpayers may treat items differently than they would if they knew that the return would be audited.

In terms of audits, a distinction must be drawn between transactions covered by information returns and those not covered by information returns. A common information return is called a Form 1099. For instance, if a tract of land is sold through a realtor, by law a 1099 is filed by the realtor reporting the sales price and the seller by TIN (taxpayer's identification number, which for an individual is the social security number). The seller gets a copy of the 1099. A person with income covered by a 1099 who does not report it, is either a fool or does not understand what a 1099 is. These are audited by computer. Years ago before this system was in place, a person might leave interest on savings accounts off his or her income tax return, and that would probably not be picked up. Now, it is almost a certainty that such an omission will be picked up by the computers.

Twice there have been efforts by the Washington, D.C., tax apparatus to extend withholding to dividends and interest. The effort in the early 1960s failed to pass Congress. Former Commissioner Caplin tells a story about a woman writing him a letter asking, "How dare you try to tax the interest on my savings accounts." He adds that she received an interesting audit. The moral? Never write a poison pen letter to the IRS, even if you think there are no possible grounds for a deficiency.

Giving information about an enemy is another matter. If you give the Service concrete information about another taxpayer, and an audit results in the collection of additional tax, the Service is authorized to pay up to 10 percent of the amount as an informer's fee.

Our income tax decreases privacy in a number of ways. Things that our ancestors would have regarded as nobody else's business are now the IRS's business. If litigated, your private matters can become part of court papers, a public record. Also, Service employees can look up various details on the computer about well-known persons or even their neighbors.

Playing the audit lottery can take a variety of forms. At one extreme is a situation in which the taxpayer cannot reasonably argue that the item should be treated as he or she did. At the other extreme is a situation in which the arguments for the taxpayer are strong and arguments to the contrary are weak. In the first type of situation, the taxpayer's position may be fraudulent. In fraud cases, the government has the burden of proof. So a case in which fraud was asserted would have to be one with strong evidence available to the government.

## An Audit Lottery Example

A deduction taken on one or more of Bill and Hillary Clinton's federal income tax returns illustrates the audit lottery. (My understanding of this situation comes from the news media.)

They were 50 percent stockholders in a corporation, usually referred to as Whitewater, and they took a deduction on their income tax return(s) for interest they paid on a debt owed by the corporation. As graduates of the Yale Law School, they probably understood that the corporation was a separate legal entity from them. They probably understood that changes in facts can change legal consequences. One or both of them should have thought, "We can deduct interest on our own debts, but can we deduct interest paid on a debt of the corporation?"

One of the truisms about the federal income tax is that it has become a monstrous complexity and applying it to a myriad of fact situations produces a vast amount of controversy. But there are, nevertheless, many simple situations where the income tax law is clear and easily applied. One of those clear rules is that you can only deduct interest paid on your own debt, not interest paid on the debt of another person. The proper result in the case of a stockholder paying interest on a debt of the corporation is that the stockholder cannot deduct the interest paid. The stockholder adds it to the cost (basis) of his stock, and the amount paid will affect the ultimate gain or loss on sale of the stock or the amount deductible if the stock becomes worthless.

If Hillary Clinton had wanted to be sure about the proper treatment of such an interest payment, how difficult would it have been for her to find out? Very simple: just ask one of the partners or associates in her law firm working in the tax area. If that person could not answer immediately, the research required would take very few minutes. There would have been no charge to her!

The possibility that Bill and Hillary Clinton are model taxpayers who carefully find out the tax law and follow the law, even when it will not save them income tax as they hoped, is so remote as to be negligible.

If Bill and Hillary Clinton knew the deduction was either doubtful or possibly improper, but they nevertheless claimed the deduction, they were playing the audit lottery. If the return were not audited (or if audited, the item not noticed by the auditing agent), they would win by saving on income tax paid.

Assume that one or both of them knew the deduction was improper, but they still claimed the deduction? That would be playing the audit lottery, but it would also be more: fraud. Fraud has to be proven by the government. Without admission by the Clintons or some discovered prior written statement by them that they knew the law and the proper treatment of interest paid on a debt owed by another person, even a suspicious agent would never think of suggesting fraud.

One of the unfortunate aspects of the income tax is that conscientious, honest taxpayers pay more than their fair share. On the other hand, the amount lost by the federal government from taxpayers playing the audit lottery must be huge. My guess would be between forty and seventy-five billion dollars a year.

# 3
# THE INCOME TAX: A CONTROVERSY-GENERATING MACHINE

The federal income tax has vast potential for generating controversies between taxpayers and the Internal Revenue Service. The actual controversies (while large in volume) fall far short of the potential controversies. For individual income taxpayers with only income subject to withholding and who use the standard deduction rather than itemize deductions, controversies are rare. Many taxpayers accept the Service's assertion of a tax deficiency, when small in amount compared to the taxpayer's net worth, rather than argue. If such taxpayers seek the advice of a tax practitioner, it may well be, "Pay it; the cost of contesting it will be more than the amount involved." Uncontested amounts paid to the Service each year to which it is not entitled, or at least arguably not entitled probably total several billion dollars, maybe as much as forty billion. Since the IRS's files are not public record, the matter cannot be studied directly by scholars. Inferences that there are errors can be drawn from the erroneous information given by IRS personnel in answering telephone inquiries. Also, there are wide variations in returns prepared by practitioners when the same facts are given to different return preparers (***Money Magazine*** and ***The Wall Street Journal*** have done this, and published the results). A large number of errors are inevitable with such a vast, complicated income tax law. While my opinion is that Congress bears most responsibility, others, including the Service, the courts, and tax practitioners, have contributed to the problem.

If a return is not audited, any potential issues will not generate a controversy. The current audit rate (under 1 percent for individuals and about 3 percent for businesses) is widely believed to be too low to be an effective deterrent to playing the audit lottery (hopefully short of fraud) on a return, because the likelihood of audit is low. Nor is it a certainty that a potential issue will arise if a return is audited. Often an advisor will tell a client: "We are in a gray area. We can argue this, and the Service can argue that. But we can probably reach a compromise with Appeals and pay 50 percent or less of the proposed additional tax."

Then there may be an audit, in which the agent doesn't see the issue. The returns of large corporations are often audited by teams of agents who work in specialized areas on which they have become experts. Perhaps the team includes an attorney. But the returns of small businesses and individuals are usually audited by a single agent. Such an agent cannot be an expert in all areas of the income tax law. Further, an agent who becomes more experienced and understands more, and also displays a good analytical mind, may be hired away from the Service by an accounting or law firm or by the tax department of some corporation.

Even though the Service conducts extensive training programs, agents are not able to comprehend all areas of taxation. During audits, many agents look into a few areas, those in which they feel comfortable, and ignore most other matters. If those areas are the ones likely to yield more dollars in deficiencies, this may be best for the Service. In effect the agent is skimming the cream, forsaking time on legal research on other matters likely to involve smaller sums of money. A detailed audit of all items involved in a particular return is a rarity.

Our federal income tax is a self-assessment system. The taxpayer files a return revealing a liability. If payment of that liability does not accompany the return, it is assessed and, without any further proceedings, the Service is authorized to initiate efforts to collect the liability. If a letter demand for payment does not result in payment, the Service has powerful weapons, such as levying on bank accounts or seizing assets and selling them at public auction. Indeed, the collection process may produce more antagonism against the Service than the audit process.

In filing a return, taxpayers and their advisors tend to resolve reasonable doubts in favor of the taxpayer. The Service's top officials assert that a taxpayer taking a position that is probably inconsistent with the Service's position on a matter should disclose that on the return. Many practitioners do not agree and do not flag the issue on the return. If there is an inquiry about the matter on audit, the only ethical choice for the taxpayer and the advisor is, of course, to respond truthfully. Indeed, intentionally false statements to the Service can lead to a criminal charge, even though the return as filed would not result in a criminal charge.

What should auditing agents do if they find a matter on which the taxpayer has resolved reasonable doubts in his or her favor? There is some argument for treatment of the item in favor of the Service, so that an additional tax may be owed. Agents are trained that it is not their job to compromise on the basis of "hazards of litigation." More experienced agents may get an "agreed" case—taxpayer signs consent to the assessment of additional tax—by not referring to their concessions in their report. (A report, a copy of which is sent to the taxpayer, is the normal conclusion of an audit.)

The taxpayer takes the initial position in filing his or her return. If audited, the burden of proof is on the taxpayer to substantiate his or her position both by the facts and legal authority. This is an inevitable rule, for the Service could not conceivably have the resources to prepare all the income tax returns for all the taxpayers or to carry the burden of proof on audits. A taxpayer who fails to keep adequate records and supporting data runs a risk of paying additional tax by default, because of inability to substantiate the return as filed.

This scheme—with taxpayers resolving doubts for themselves and auditing agent resolving doubts for the Service—results in controversy once the agent sees an issue. A taxpayer who elects to contest the agent's report may file a protest within thirty days and ask for a hearing before the appeals office. The appeals office exists to resolve these disputes. Attorneys in the district counsel's office are available to assist the appeals officers. These people are mostly experienced and able. They resolve about 90 percent of disputes that reach them. This helps keep the federal income tax functioning. Were it not for them, the courts would be in even worse trouble.

If compromise with the appeals office fails, taxpayers, of course, can litigate. They have two choices of where to litigate. In the U.S. Tax Court, payment is not required until a final decision is reached. If the taxpayer pays the amount and seeks a refund, he or she can litigate in either a federal district court or the U.S. Claims Court. Only in a district court can a taxpayer have a jury trial.

An audit can be stressful for a taxpayer. Typically it comes unexpectedly. It can be disruptive of the taxpayer's affairs and of his employees. The awesome power of the federal government may become apparent. The auditing agent can look into the records of banks, stock brokers, and others with whom the taxpayer has had business or investment contacts.

I believe the quality of agents has declined during my lifetime. It can be argued, however, that many agent inadequacies are the result of the increase in the length of the code, regulations, and other authorities, plus their complexity. Tax practitioners also are having trouble coping with the current federal income tax. A former student of mine, now an appeals officer, stated that he was appalled by the poor quality of reports by revenue agents.

Auditing agents are aware of the large number of complaints about the Service. They may become unduly sensitive to any perceived criticism of the Service or them. This has been called a "siege mentality at the IRS" ( ***Financial World***, Oct. 27, 1992). If an auditing agent believes the taxpayer or the taxpayer's representative has belittled the Service (or the agent), the agent's judgment may be distorted and the likelihood of a favorable report for the taxpayer reduced. Auditing agents typically believe they have a job to do, and that it is important for them to protect the revenue of the federal government. The appeals office and district counsel's office both are dependent upon audit in various ways, such as supplementary reports and expert witnesses in trials. The agent may inform the appeals officer that the taxpayer or the taxpayer's representative was rude and offensive. The taxpayer then will have less chance of obtaining an optimum settlement from appeals.

There can be no doubt that there is much antagonism by some taxpayers and tax practitioners against the Service, and by some Service personnel against taxpayers. Many taxpayers cheat on the income tax—"about one-fifth of respondents in a national survey admitted underreporting income or overstating deductions" ***Income Tax Cheating*** (Kinsey and Smith American Bar Foundation, Chicago, 1987, p. 1). Service personnel realize this, and unfortunately, when a taxpayer deals with Service personnel, he does not bear a mark showing whether he is honest or dishonest. IRS agents are at times berated, threatened and even attacked by taxpayers. IRS agents may become overbearing if they suspect hostility or dishonesty. Of course, whether the antagonism comes first from the agent or the taxpayer, the other is likely to react with hostility. Agents in such situations are likely to look for many items to adjust to increase tax liability. Some of their positions may be unreasonable. If a proposed deficiency is so large that it will strain the taxpayer's ability to pay, the taxpayer may become desperate. This creates yet another story of the Service's unreasonableness and adds to the siege mentality of the Service and the fear of the Service by many taxpayers.

There is much agony inherent in the income tax. Congress, by adding complexities, adds to the conflict and antagonism. During my professional life, the Internal Revenue Code has inexorably become more complex and the regulations longer. In 1950 I carried the regulations to the U.S. Tax Court in my briefcase—it was a small book. The regulations now are about twenty times as long and in the Commerce Clearing House printing fill six thick volumes. The makeup of the Congress and the way it operates generates more and more complexity. The multiplicity of tax reform acts is an indication of Congress's inability to achieve reform. The Tax Reform Act of 1986, however, did accomplish a very important objective by ending tax shelters as they had existed and lowering rates. Lower rates result in decreased motivation for tax evasion and avoidance. (See chapter 11 for a discussion of the damage done by the 1986 Act to real estate values in many areas of the United States when tax shelters were ended.)

Compromise is practiced by the Congress. If two relatively simple positions on a tax matter are represented by powerful opposing groups, the likely result is complicated legislation that is an effort, to some degree, to placate both groups. This is in line with the growing tradition in politics of trying to be all things to all people. Indeed, I believe many of our best people are unwilling to offer themselves as candidates for elective office or for appointment to federal positions that require Congressional approval (remember Robert Bork and Zoe Baird). Indiana has three members of Congress of undoubted integrity: Lee Hamilton, Andy Jacobs, and Dick Lugar. It may be significant that both Hamilton and Jacobs are in districts safe for their party (although even they had close races in 1994) and thus are under less strain to raise campaign funds and campaign long and strenuously.

Another defect of the Congress in the tax area is that much of the staff of the Joint Committee on Taxation, which serves as staff to both the Senate Finance Committee and the Ways and Means Committee, as well as the separate staffs of those two committees, are younger people, not long out of academic life. Few, if any, have had experience in the field representing either taxpayers or the Service. Thus, they lack understanding of how difficult it is for those in the field to handle the complexities the Congress enacts. There is probably specialization within the staff of the Joint Committee, so no one is forced to deal with complexities all across the income tax, as practitioners in smaller firms (either law or accounting) do. Staff members of the Joint Committee who helps create complexities in such areas as international taxation, qualified pension plans, corporate taxation and so on, soon develop a readily marketable skill. They may be hired by a big law firm or a big accounting firm, in which specialization has developed to cope with the monstrous complication, the income tax has become. I said to one attorney from a large Chicago firm that specialization was necessary for tax practitioners to cope with the income tax. He said, "You're right. We have two attorneys who work on nothing other than the income taxation of bankruptcy and insolvency."

Sympathy is called for, not only for tax practitioners, but also for auditing agents who conduct solo audits. Because of turnover, caused in part by low morale, auditing agents are likely to be young and relatively inexperienced. Although they have a degree in accounting, their grades were probably in the lower part of their class, and they have difficulty dealing with the complexity.

The Internal Revenue Service deserves blame for the income tax problem, but the Congress also deserves some criticism. Congress creates a monstrosity and does not adequately fund the Service to carry out its function; for example, there needs to be an audit level high enough to be a reasonably effective deterrent against playing the audit lottery. Indeed, the Internal Revenue Service is one of the better U.S. agencies, according to ***Financial World*** (Oct. 27, 1992), in an article rating ten U.S. agencies. The Internal Revenue Service received a B+ rating, the highest of any of the agencies. Whenever rating the Internal Revenue Service, an allowance should be made for what Congress has created for it to administer.

Say Congress substantially increased funding for Internal Revenue. This is arguably rational, because the Service produces revenue in excess of the marginal dollars appropriated. Assume increased pay for Service personnel, maybe even employing retired tax accountants and tax attorneys. Perhaps even give a contingent fee for taxes collected from deficiencies (informers can receive up to 10 percent of the income tax received as a result of an informer's tip; why not auditing agents?). I've been asking experienced tax practitioners for years about what would happen if the above occurred, followed by my own prediction, "Within a year or so, there would be enough proposed deficiencies to impair the credit worthiness of a large number of businesses in the country." I have never had one person contradict my prediction.

Almost all banks ask about tax claims in an application for a loan. The proposed deficiencies taken to appeals on average are for an amount much larger than the amount settled for by appeals. But if a loan officer at a bank knows that a proposed deficiency is for $200,000, that is the amount used in evaluating a loan application.

**Personal or Business Expense**

Some income tax rules are perpetual generators of controversy. Language in the Internal revenue Code is often general, although sometimes agonizingly long in detail, because those who draft it cannot anticipate the myriad situations that will arise from the general concept. The rule that personal, family, and living expenses are not deductible, for example, while business expenses are deductible, is a huge source of controversy. Here is an example to show how factual situations make it difficult to apply this seemingly simple rule of law. Say a sole proprietor, who normally eats from a brown bag for lunch, takes the purchasing agent from a potential customer to lunch at the most expensive restaurant in town and lands a sales contract.

Now food is an essential living expense, but business permeates the luncheon. The profit from such a sale will be subject to income taxation, and the businessperson has incurred an expense much beyond his or her normal expense for lunch. In this situation, the expense should be deductible. However, the deductibility of the cost of business meals creates opportunities for abuse. For instance, two friends who regularly have lunch together—if each is in business—could swap paying for lunch and have the cost reduced by the tax benefit. If they are both employees on expense accounts, their lunch won't cost them anything. And if they have a three-martini lunch, they won't get much work done that afternoon.

Let's use this business meal issue to consider (1) the investigative powers of the Internal Revenue Service, and (2) the complexity of the Internal Revenue Code. The investigative powers of the IRS are broad, both with regard to taxpayers' records and those of third persons, such as banks and customers or suppliers. If the agent were to inquire into each business meal, the process would be incredibly time consuming.

Congress's approach in this case has been to adopt a rule that only 50 percent of the cost of business meals is deductible (justice on the average?). Such an arbitrary rule offends persons who have legitimate expenses, and perhaps motivates them to engage in petty cheating on other items. This 50 percent denial of a deduction for business meals only comes into play after the application of a number of other rules designed to prevent improper deductions.

To illustrate how harshly this 50 percent rule can operate, consider two partners (each an equal partner) or an S corporation with two 50 percent stockholders. This business sells a product line (say plumbing supplies) and has had excellent growth and follows the practice of reimbursing salesmen in full for business meals for customers (or potential customers). The partnership does not pay income tax, but each 50 percent owner reports one half of the income. Here the 50 percent amount disallowed as a deduction increases the income of the owners, despite the fact they will not receive the cost of the meals, and the full reimbursement of the salesman reflects a business judgment that the business meal aids sales.

## Independent Contractor or Employee

Another bothersome issue is whether a person rendering services for another is an independent contractor or an employee. The greater control the one receiving the services has over the one rendering the services, the more likely it is that the relationship will be "found" to be employer-employee. An employer must withhold income tax and social security taxes (the latter the employer matches in amount) from the employee's compensation, but not from the pay of an independent contractor. The independent contractor by law is supposed to pay estimated income tax and self-employment tax. Penalties, if IRS says "employer/employee," can be vicious. This is a frequent source of pain for small businessmen having trouble with their cash flow. The motivation of the business person is to claim independent contractor status. Thus a taxicab company might change its practices and make what had historically been an employment relationship into a leasing arrangement. I have even heard of a lawyer contending his secretary was an independent contractor. Disputes over employee–independent contractor issues probably number into tens of thousands each year, and if the IRS had more resources could become hundreds of thousands.

## Contrary to Public Policy

A doctrine that caused trouble in earlier years was that a deduction for an expense could be denied because it was "contrary to public policy." The president of a coal company in southwestern Virginia in the years after World War II, when there were frequent shortages of railway coal cars, gave whiskey, hams, turkeys and so on to railway train crew members at Easter, Memorial Day, the Fourth of July, Labor Day, Thanksgiving, and Christmas. Lo, his company received coal cars during shortages, while other mines got few or none. Knowing that "commercial bribery" was then an active concern under the "contrary to public policy" doctrine, I asked the president how those gifts were handled. He said, "We put it in the lubrication account." Cases and regulations have reduced disputes in this area, and taxpayers may have learned to be resourceful in avoiding problems. When Congress imposes rules widely perceived as unjust, burying details in the books, as the coal company did, will ensue. The Service cannot do a detailed audit of every taxpayer.

## Debt or Equity

Corporations can deduct interest paid on borrowed capital (debt), but not dividends paid on stock (equity). Often the revenue agent will assert that instruments that are debt on their face are in substance equity. Congress in 1969 enacted Section 385 of the Internal Revenue Code authorizing regulations in an attempt to reduce such disputes. Proposed regulations were issued in March 1980 (more than ten years later) and withdrawn on December 30, 1981, after a flood of criticism. New proposed regulations were issued the same day, but these were also withdrawn in July 1983. Trying to reduce these intractable, multifaceted factual questions to certainty is an illusion.

The rule that interest on debt is deductible encourages corporations to have more bonds and less stock. This is unfortunate, because it makes the corporations vulnerable during recessions. Payment of interest is mandatory (indeed, making it optional encourages the Service to argue it is not debt), while dividends payments can be suspended.

It was this deductibility of interest that encouraged hostile takeovers of publicly traded corporations in the 1980s, using "junk bonds." Many of those corporations unfortunately ended up in bankruptcy.

## Constructive Dividends

The Service may argue that a payment deducted by a corporation should be treated "constructively" as a dividend and not be deducted. For instance, salary paid to a stockholder-officer may be said to exceed a "reasonable" salary. Only the amount that is reasonable can be deducted as a salary, but the excess is still treated as income to the stockholder because it is a constructive dividend. Such disputes are common in closely held family businesses that are incorporated.

**International Taxation**

While some factual issues arise in many contexts, others occur in a limited area. An example of this is transfer pricing in international taxation. A foreign corporation with a U.S. subsidiary may sell products to it at high prices, so that the U.S. subsidiary show low profits on resale. The Service may challenge the price as not being an "arms-length" price—this is called "transfer pricing." A similar issue may arise involving a U.S. corporation owning a manufacturing subsidiary in Puerto Rico (with tax and other advantages granted for economic development).

These cases are so complex and time consuming that the Service is fighting a losing cause; it can only audit and litigate a small percentage of such returns. I talked to an appeals officer in Indianapolis who worked on such a case involving Eli Lilly. The records in that case were moved to court on pallets by a forklift.

The Internal Revenue Service has succeeded in reducing controversies about transfer pricing by getting advanced pricing agreements with multinational corporations.

Although we won't consider in detail other factual issues that cause many controversies between citizens and the IRS, here is a partial list of some of the common areas (the list could be much, much longer):

1. Has a corporation unreasonably accumulated earnings instead of paying dividends? (A penalty tax applies.)
2. Was there a profit motive? (If none, a loss cannot be deducted.)
3. What is the fair market value of property?

4. Is an amount at risk? (This is important in the tax shelter area.)
5. Is an activity passive? (Certain passive activity losses are not currently deductible.)
6. To whom is income taxed? (For instance,is income taxed to a high-bracket parent or a low-bracket child.)
7. What is one's home? (This is important for purposes of deducting business travel expenses.)
8. When is a home office expense deductible?
9. When, if ever, is a bad debt deductible?
10. When is a security worthless?
11. Is an item a gift (not income) or income?
12. Is a transaction bonafide?
13. Was there a business purpose?
14. Is a cost an expense or a capital expenditure?
15. Is property held for sale in the ordinary course of business, or does it qualify for a capital gain treatment?
16. What is support for determining a dependency deduction?
17. Was there a claim of right? (If received under a claim of right, an item can be income even though it is later repaid.)
18. Was there an involuntary conversion?
19. Were meals and lodging furnished for the convenience of the employer?
20. Was there a partial liquidation?
21. What is cost?
22. What is a medical expense?
23. Is discharge of indebtedness a gift or income?
24. Can a corporate entity be ignored?
25. Was there a cash equivalent payment? (Income-in-kind.)

26. Is there an economic interest? (This is an issue in percentage depletion.)
27. Has there been economic performance? (This is an issue in accrual accounting.)
28. What educational expenses are deductible?
29. Is this evasion (fraud) or avoidance (good tax planning)?
30. Is one an innocent spouse? (Therefore the person is not liable for the fraud of the other spouse.)
31. Is this a sale or lease?
32. Are certain properties of like kind?
33. Is there material participation?
34. What is a moving expense?
35. Is a business expense "ordinary and necessary"?
36. Was there negligence? (This is significant for purposes of a penalty.)

# 4
# COMPLEXITIES OF OUR PRESENT INCOME TAX

A net income tax in effect incorporates the subject of accounting into our income tax law. Determining net income (or profit) is one major function of accounting. But accounting is difficult subject matter. This is one reason our federal income tax is inherently complex. Some of these accounting complexities are discussed below.

Accounting periods are necessary; the period chosen for tax purposes is a year. But rules are needed for what year may be used. For example, shall only the calendar year be permitted? If a fiscal year is permitted, on what day of the month may a fiscal year end?

Many transactions occur over more than a year, and rules are needed to determine the year or years in which an item will be accounted for. An example is a partial payment in advance to a manufacturer to produce a quantity of goods to order. These goods are to be produced over the next two years with delivery early in the third year after the year of payment.

Another example: An owner of land enters into a contract to sell the land. Payments of both principal and interest are made over many years, and the deed is delivered at the time of the final payment. This example can be further complicated if the contract buyer, because of financial difficulties, agrees with the contract seller for a mutual release, with the contract seller keeping the payments already made. Complexity is inherent in accounting for transactions occurring over more than one year.

There is enough authority on tax accounting that a multi-volume treatise could be written on tax accounting, which in some respects differs from the generally accepted accounting principles (GAAP) used in the business world.

Inventories are a major feature of both GAAP and tax accounting. Manufacturers, wholesalers, and retailers must use inventories in order to reflect their net income clearly. The basic formulas for using inventories are (1) gross sales receipts less cost of goods sold equals gross income, and (2) cost of goods sold is opening inventory plus purchases less closing inventory. For a manufacturer of many different products, manufacturing costs are used instead of purchases. This gets into cost accounting, a difficult and advanced field of accounting. Not even for a wholesaler or retailer is inventory simple, because freight, insurance, and discounts are relevant. Furthermore, since costs of the same goods fluctuate (generally upward), accounting conventions are needed; the most widely known are FIFO (first in, first out) and LIFO (last in, first out). These are also considered in the discussion of the relationship of inflation to the federal income tax.

Tax accounting requires a distinction between capital expenditures and those costs taken into account entirely within a single year. Accountants speak in terms of "expensing" (entire cost deducted in one year) and "capitalizing" (cost treated as purchase of an asset). If capitalized, the next question becomes when, if ever, the cost will be recovered to reflect the "net" aspect of the income tax. For an asset with a perpetual life such as land, the cost will be recovered only as a "basis" when and if the land is sold; that is, only the profit or gain is reported as gross income, not the whole sales price. For assets with a limitied useful life, such as buildings, machinery and equipment, the cost must be deducted over a period of time, and this deduction is called depreciation.

Determining which expenditures should be capitalized and which should be expensed is a never-ending source of controversy between businesses and the Service.

Depreciation during the first forty years of the income tax was relatively simple compared to what it has become over the last forty years. Straight line depreciation was the norm. If a factory bought a machine with a predicted useful life of ten years, 10 percent of the cost would be deducted each year as depreciation. With the inflation from World War II and the succeeding years, business leaders argued that depreciation based on historical cost was unfair, and in fact, the income tax was operating as a levy on capital not on "net" income. (I agree with this position.) They argued that depreciation should be based upon replacement cost.

The response was not to adopt replacement cost depreciation, but rather "accelerated" depreciation and shorter useful lives. In accelerated depreciation the total deduction over the useful life is limited to the cost but with larger deductions in the earlier years and smaller deductions in the later years. This has a tendency to encourage businesses to make new investment in depreciable assets, thus stimulating the economy. The sooner a deduction can be taken, the greater the present value of the tax benefit from the deduction. In a period of high inflation accompanied by high interest rates, the present value of a deduction in the twentieth year in the future (using a twenty-year useful life) would be so small relatively that it would have little impact on a business decision to buy new machinery and equipment.

The trend toward shorter useful lives and faster depreciation reached a peak with the 1981 Economic Recovery Tax Act (ERTA). Starting in 1982 the trend was reversed and the treatment of depreciation now is a source of complaint by business taxpayers.

The treatment of depreciation by the 1981 Act was considered by some too favorable to business; they called it a loophole or a tax preference or a tax expenditure. Others supported accelerated depreciation as stimulating the economy. The long economic recovery starting in 1982 could be used to support the latter position, as do arguments similar to those for replacement cost depreciation.

An illustration of the complexity of the income tax: A man had bought some corporate bonds, which the original owner had bought at a discount (a price lower than the face amount or the maturity amount). That discount could have resulted from a below-market interest rate or even no interest (often called zero coupon bonds).

Congress requires that even cash method taxpayers report portions of "original issue discount" on corporate bonds annually, even if they are not the original owner of the bonds. The man asked his tax accountant about reporting this original issue discount. His accountant said that he would just make a guess. The actual computation was difficult, time-consuming, and costly. Also, getting information about the amount of original discount could be almost impossible.

There are areas of complexity that would be difficult to explain to even the most intelligent person without special tax training, such as international taxation, pension and profit sharing, taxation of insurance companies, corporate reorganizations (mergers, split-ups, etc.), and oil and gas taxation.

Qualified pension plans, which affect tens of millions of people, deserve some comment.

Almost all large businesses have qualified employee retirement plans, while only a small percentage of small businesses do. Why is that? Complexity, cost, and constant change. Complexity means specialists charge more. There are fewer of them (in a sub-specialty within tax law), and they have to make a huge investment in time to master the complexities. Typically a tax lawyer, a tax accountant, and an employee benefit firm (including actuaries) are involved in establishing a qualified pension plan, so there are more professionals to pay. Constant change means constant updating and more cost. Thus most small businesses do not have pension plans; they cost too much.

On November 19, 1993, during the IRS-Bar Association Regional Liaison Meeting held in Cincinnati, a panel consisting of two attorneys specializing in qualified pension plans and the IRS Chief for Employee Plans in Cincinnati discussed pension plans. The minutes show that one attorney noted that noncompliance in the employee plans area is an epidemic. He speculated that virtually every plan could probably be disqualified. The IRS specialist did not challenge that statement, and the overall tenor of the discussion made it clear that statement is correct. The IRS works quietly for correction of mistakes rather than ruling the plan unqualified and imposing the drastic consequences.

We will see in chapter 14 that the IRS imposed deficiencies for trivial failures to comply fully with the intricacies of the complex rules on charitable deferred giving. There Congress, after fifteen years, enacted permanent legislation permitting reformation to eliminate relatively small defects, thereby avoiding paying additional tax. In contrast, in the pension-plan area the IRS, on its own, permits modifications without explicit congressional action. Why is this so?

The answer is that the IRS, in a way, is like a predator; it prefers a lone prey. This is not to say that revenue agents are predators, but they do have a job to do. Their job is to locate persons who owe additional income tax, as they interpret the code, regulations, manuals, and so forth. A single taxpayer faces the awesome power Congress has given the IRS. If the taxpayer has no particular connections and lacks funds to hire a competent attorney and litigate, he or she will be hopelessly outgunned by a single revenue agent. That was the situation for taxpayers faced with the absurdly complex charitable deferred giving scheme Congress enacted.

Few individuals will do as Sergeant York did in World War I—fight about fifty or sixty enemy soldiers and march the thirty-eight still alive back as prisoners all alone! The IRS is no Sergeant York; it doesn't get in fights it is likely to lose. To take on a qualified pension plan is to take on all the participants in the plan—ranging from a few score in the smaller plans to hundreds of thousands in the largest plans. Can you imagine what would happen if the IRS notified all the employees of even a medium-sized company that they had to pay income tax for the past three years on all their employer's contributions to their pension plan? Realistically, the IRS selectively elects not to enforce some provisions of the Internal Revenue Code against strong foes, while proceeding against weak foes under other provisions.

Complexity is a form of discrimination. If a violation of a tax complexity is detected by a revenue agent, the individual is at a disadvantage. But, on the other hand, if a taxpayer violates a tax complexity, a revenue agent is unlikely to understand the complexity and the violation will probably go undetected. Thus, the Treasury Department has been its own enemy in persuading Congress to enact the huge array of complexities that exist in the Internal Revenue Code.

The Alternative Minimum Tax is a major complication. It was enacted in 1969; in effect it is a tax upon successful tax planning, but it is erratic in its application. If the regular income tax is less than the alternative minimum tax, the taxpayer pays an additional amount to bring the total up to the amount of the alternative minimum. It is a symptom of a sick tax system, and unfortunately it may have to be paid by a taxpayer with no net income but rather with a loss.

The position against complexity and in support of simplicity was well-stated by Sam M. Gibbons, ranking Democrat on the Ways and Means Committee, in testimony before that committee on June 7, 1995:

> Both individuals and businesses resent and complain about the level of complexity of the current tax system. Taxpayers worry that they are being unfairly taxed and that others have found ways to avoid the tax. Extensive and lucrative industries of lawyers, accountants, and tax preparers spend countless hours and unbounded energy helping taxpayers through the maze of complexity to minimize their tax liabilities. A simpler tax system would free up these resources to en-

> gage in more productive economic enterprises. A simpler system would be better understood by the average citizen and, thus, would avoid the ill will and skepticism generated by the current system. A simpler system would improve compliance and streamline administration.

Gibbons favors abolishing the income tax and replacing it with a value-added tax (VAT). (See Chapter 21 on the Nunn-Domenici USA Tax Proposal for a discussion of VATs.)

It is significant that both Bill Archer, chairman of Ways and Means, and Sam Gibbons, ranking Democrat on Ways and Means, both favor abolishing the federal income tax. If we abolish the income tax, we also abolish its complexities. Replacing it with a national sales tax would be the simplest possible replacement.

## 5
## "OPPORTUNITIES" FOR THOSE DEALING IN CASH

The income tax is a self-assessment system with the taxpayer filing a return that discloses (assesses) his liability. Taxpayers are under an obligation to keep records that show their income and expenses. If taxpayers receive cash income and omit some of it from their records, or keep no records, and also omit it from reported income, the Service can detect the income only in a small percentage of cases (for example, when there are regular deposits of cash in excess of recorded receipts). However, an intelligent taxpayer (although dishonest) realizes that the Service's power to reach bank records is one of its major audit resources (also a major cost and annoyance to the banks). So cash omitted from income is typically expended directly as cash for consumption, travel abroad, or minor assets not leaving a paper record as opposed to purchases of real estate and securities. Cash may also be accumulated, ultimately to be "laundered."

The Service has developed some ingenious methods of "reconstructing" income. These include the net worth method (increase in net worth plus nondeductible expenditures is net income); bank deposits method (deposits as income less deductible expenditures paid by check, plus estimated undeposited cash); and the expenditures method.

But these methods are inexact and less persuasive when the amounts are small relative to reported income and the results are not consistent over a period of time. and they have several drawbacks. The methods are enormously time consuming, and the Service is understaffed for the task assigned it. Congress is unwilling to fund the Service adequately. Already members of

Congress receive a large volume of complaints about the actions of the Service, some justified, some not. Members of Congress realize that increased appropriations would increase the complaints. There would be more audits and more assessed additional tax. There is, of course, a benefit to incumbent Congressmen from "constituent services" in this area. Particularly if a member of the House Ways and Means Committee, Senate Finance Committee, or an Appropriations Committee makes a pointed complaint for a constituent or for a non-constituent large contributor, the Service may back away from a sound position out of fear of revenge by a Congressman in a key position.

While the Service and Treasury for many years contended that "fraudulently" omitted income was small in amount and the likelihood of detection and punishment high, about twenty years ago, as publications about the underground economy began appearing, the truth began to be admitted by the Service and the Treasury Department: there is a large gap between revenue collected and the revenue which should be collected. The amount is currently estimated at about $127 billion a year. and many think it is much larger. Cash omissions from income are a major cause of this "revenue gap," and even with greatly increased audit activity could only be somewhat reduced, not eliminated.

Thus a practical consequence of the income tax is that the taxpayers who have income only from monitored sources pay more than their fair share of the cost (and waste) of the federal government. Monitored sources include wages, dividends, interest, and other payments covered by 1099s (information returns by payors on amounts paid to payees). Prostitutes, drug dealers, illegal gamblers (and maybe even legal casinos), sole proprietors rendering services, and very small businesses where only family members handle cash can pay much less than their fair share. Others who are in a position to underpay substantially include owners of laundromats, coin-vending machines, limousine services, car wrecking/parts, car towing, taxi companies, equipment rentals, and junk/scrap metal businesses.

This incentive to evade taxes is a major argument against the income tax, and it is inherent and largely irremediable. A tax with a correlation to consumer expenditures would be fairer. An expenditures tax with reported income as the starting point, as some have suggested, would retain the opportunity to take advantage for those dealing in cash. Such an expenditures tax might start with taxable income, subtract savings, and add back withdrawals of savings as income. Such a proposal retains all the disadvantages of the self-assessment system now in use.

# 6
# DISCRIMINATION AGAINST SMALL BUSINESSES

The discrimination against small businesses results largely from the complexity of the income tax law. This complexity has two aspects: difficult to understand concepts and a staggering volume of provisions. Congress is the primary perpetrator of this complexity. It is becoming increasingly difficult to understand how and why the American people—with an earlier history of freedom and individualism—tolerate the situation.

The complexity weighs heavily on small businesses. They must collect the tax, including social security taxes, for the government from their employees at their expense. Then they must carefully manage their cash flow. Congress has mandated a first priority to deposit the "withheld" employment taxes in the banking system for the government. If they pay some urgent expense first, and then fall behind on depositing the taxes, they face severe penalties.

Service personnel tend to have a strong emotional reaction to small businesses that are delinquent in paying "withheld" employment taxes, viewing this as akin to robbery. The language Congress uses in this area causes confusion. By law, the "withheld" taxes are called a trust fund. But no discrete, segregated trust fund exists until the employer makes the deposit in the banking system. The term "withheld" is inaccurate: what has happened is that by law Congress has ordered an employer to pay part of a debt to someone else (wages owed to an employee) to the IRS. The employee receives a credit against his income tax liability and to his social security account. The social security tax imposed upon the employer equal to the amount "withheld" from the employee's wages is, of course, initially the employer's debt.

Collecting taxes for the government at their expense is only the start of the small business's need to cope with the income tax. Decisions about the organization and operation of the business, unless made with adequate understanding of the income tax consequences, can result in large increases in tax costs and even in failure of the business. The cost to a small business of getting advice from lawyers and accountants is substantial. In a highly technical areas, such as qualified retirement plans (which Congress changes constantly) the costs are prohibitively high. It is common knowledge among tax professionals that many small businesses have either abandoned such plans or decided not to start a retirement plan.

These costs are economically unproductive and many small businesses, of course, offset the cost by tax avoidance and evasion. But do we do ourselves a service by a tax system with a strong incentive for dishonesty?

## 7
## INFLATION AND THE INCOME TAX

One fundamental aspect of the federal income tax is that items are measured by dollars, with the assumption being that the dollar is a constant measure of value. That is false. For half a century we have had inflation and a dollar of declining value in real purchasing power. While the rate of inflation has at times been faster (Truman, Johnson, Carter) and at times slower (Eisenhower, Reagan), the trend has persisted. Thus our federal income tax, by using the dollar in measuring items, involves a major distortion in the measurement of income that would not be present in a tax on current consumption expenditures, for example..

There are winners and losers from this impact of inflation on income tax liabilities. In general—those investing in real estate, stock equities, and certain tangibles such as art or antiques, especially those highly leveraged with debt when all interest was fully deductible—have been winners. Those holding fixed dollar investments, such as bonds, savings accounts, and cash- surrender-value life insurance (although favorable tax treatment tended to offset this last) were losers. When an informed person buys a corporate bond, he or she makes a judgment that the interest rate is high enough to cover the rate of inflation and still leave an amount as real interest. Neither the bond holder nor the corporation has any significant ability to control the rate of inflation. If adequate disclosure has been made available by the corporation, a fair arms length transaction has occurred. But if the United States government is the issuer of the bonds, and it has the power to cause higher inflation, then a moral question exists:

Doesn't the U.S. government by causing higher inflation cheat the people who showed trust in it? With inflation, bondholders lose purchasing power. But by law taxpayers cannot deduct losses due to inflation.

Conceivably a comprehensive scheme of adjustment for inflation (similar to the indexing of personal exemptions and bracket widths brought in under President Reagan) could be enacted. Such a scheme would be complicated, and the bill as introduced undoubtedly would be mutilated in the congressional process.

The U.S. government is the net winner from the combination of inflation and the net income tax. For example, capital gains are overstated since they are in part illusory; bondholders have real losses that are not deductible; higher interest rates—if the stated interest rate is nine percent and inflation is five percent, the real interest rate is four percent—yield more income subject to tax; depreciation on business property is understated and profits thereby overstated; inflationary increases in inventory costs produce nominal income, especially if FIFO is used; and, finally, if businesses are able to maintain the same percentage of gross profit on prices increased by inflation, there will be more nominal business income to tax. This increase in revenue to the federal government encourages the big spenders in Congress: they believe there will always be more revenue to cover their profligacy. The sad fact is that for each dollar of increased revenue the Congress increases spending by more than a dollar. Indeed, one study showed $1.65 of spending for each dollar of increased revenue, and another $1.59. In other words, the U.S. government and the big spenders in Congress have their bread buttered on the side of a net income tax combined with inflation.

This increase in revenue from the net income tax combined with inflation can be viewed as an automatic tax. Congress does not have to enact it and incur possible political punishment. Thus Congress is rewarded for causing inflation by gaining more revenue for more vote buying with public funds, and the circle goes on and on. The Swiss, Germans, Japanese, Koreans, Taiwanese, and others have the power to stop this. Ultimately they will realize it isn't wise to keep shipping money to a poorly governed country to cover its spendthrift budget deficits and trade deficits. When that happens we will all pay for the lack of integrity of our Congresses. (My opinions are about the pre-1995 Congress; it is too early to reach conclusions about the post-1994 Congress. Statements by Bill Archer [chairman, Ways and Means], Dick Armey [majority leader in the House], and Dick Lugar in the Senate are encouraging.)

The United States is in a precarious situation: savings are so low that they cover only a small portion of our combined budget and trade deficits; the rest is financed outside the country. It is true that the deficit now in relation to gross national product is smaller than at some times in the past, such as at the end of World War II. But that was at the end of an extraordinary and vastly expensive event. It is true also that in computing the deficit, capital expenditures are not deleted. But even if we capitalize and depreciate, we merely move expenditures forward a few years. Unless we are willing to sell off and privatize the postal system, for example, why shouldn't the cost of a new post office (usually built because the congressman from that district is on the postal sub-committee) be charged against the deficit? For many purposes, cash flow rather than net profit is the most significant matter.

## 8
## CONGRESS'S RECORD

A history of Congress's record on income taxation would be monumental. Here I will explain a few actions by Congress, often affecting large numbers of people, in which Congress has enacted unfair, discriminatory, or unduly complicated provisions.

I call many of these actions "unprincipled," by which I mean that fair minded persons with an adequate understanding of the income tax laws would find the provision objectionable. This is not to call all of the members of Congress unprincipled. Most members are aware of and understand very few income tax provisions; sometimes none of them understands a particular proposed provision.

To a significant extent the staff of the Joint Committee on Taxation is in control of writing income tax laws. It has a permanent staff, serving both the Ways and Means Committee and the Senate Finance Committee, with assistance from the Treasury Department. A major defect of the staff of the Joint Committee is that, while crowded with bright young recent academics, such as attorneys, accountants, and economists, the staff lacks persons with experience outside Washington, D.C., in the day-to-day auditing of income tax returns and settlement efforts and litigation rising out of disputes about correct tax liability.

In the following chapters I will use to illustrate Congress's dismal record in the income tax: capital gains, stock options, tax shelters, 1986 TRA transition rules, percentage depletion, deferred charitable giving and the marriage penalty.

## 9
## CAPITAL GAINS AND LOSSES

The present treatment of capital gains and losses is unfair in several ways. A capital gain is computed using the original cost in dollars as the base. If the dollar has declined in purchasing power, there is an illusory gain. For example, if an asset was bought for $1,000 and sold for $2,000, and if the dollar has lost half of its purchasing power, the taxpayer has no gain at all in purchasing power. Nevertheless, under current law, he or she has a $1,000 "gain" which is taxed as ordinary income subject to a 28 percent ceiling. President Reagan proposed indexing cost (or basis) for inflation, eliminating this illusory gain. The majority party in the Congress, then led in the Senate by George Mitchell, the self-proclaimed advocate for fairness, refused to pass it. But is it fair to tax as gain an amount that is not really a gain?

The taxation of capital losses under current law is also unfair. Capital losses may be deducted from capital gains, but a deduction from ordinary income for losses in excess of gains is limited to $3,000. While there is a carryover of capital losses not deducted to future years, up to $3,000 of losses may be discarded for each year and permanently lost as a possible deduction.

A fundamental aspect of our net income tax is that an individual has income only after recovering costs. Here Congress discriminates against taxpayers by not allowing them to recover all their costs by deducting all their capital losses. Further, because of inflation, their losses are really larger when computed in terms of lost purchasing power. It is likely that many of the people with capital losses are not the same people as those who have capital gains. An example is a person who has his or her account churned (recommending many sales and reinvestments to earn more commisions) by a stockbroker or a person who makes over-priced investments in low-priced stock, precious stones, or metals sold by con men over the telephone. Is it fair that they can't fully deduct their losses?

What is the impact upon investment in new plants and equipment of taxing capital gains at close to the rates on ordinary income? Generally a new business that raises venture capital will operate as a corporation. Small businesses, not the corporate giants, have been the source of increased employment over the last twenty years. A dominant factor in the price level of corporate stocks is earnings, which in financial news are an after-tax amount.

For a new venture, or one selling stock to the public for the first time, the prospects for future earnings move potential investors to buy. But there is a 34 percent (35 percent for larger corporations) corporate income tax which diminishes earnings. Dividends are likely to be low if the business is succeeding and growing, because growth calls for retaining earnings to finance the growth. These retained earnings tend to increase the stock price for the business. If the investor sells, his or her gain will be taxed at 28 percent. An investor would be more likely to invest in such a venture if the gain were taxed at, say, 15 percent.

There is more to say. Chronic and huge budget deficits absorb much of the funds available for investment. This reduces investment in plants and equipment, which would create jobs.

Taxation of capital gains at rates almost as high as ordinary income harms the economy in another way. Ideally an investor who has an unrealized gain on an investment should sell to reinvest in another stock that has better prospects for future growth. The capital gains tax, however, discourages selling, especially since much of the gain is illusory. This lock-in effect is more pronounced for the elderly with long-term investments. At their death, their heirs get a new base of fair-market value, which means no gain and no tax from selling the stock soon after death of the owner. Thus there is no incentive to move to new and more promising investments and the prospects for employment are reduced.

Risk taking is another aspect of a capital investment, which merits favorable tax treatment for those investing in productive enterprise. One of the most prominent features of the more advanced economies is the amount of capital invested per employee. With rare exceptions, an individual working for an unrelated person expects compensation. A wage earner or a salaried person is not risking capital but merely rendering services. But one who buys stock in a new venture is taking a risk of losing capital, just as the wage earner is when he goes to Las Vegas. Since risk taking by investing in new ventures is a gain for our economy, that investor merits a lower tax rate on any gain as an incentive to invest.

There is one disadvantage in favorable treatment of capital gains. It complicates the federal income tax law by numerous provisions attempting to draw the line between ordinary income and capital gains. But that isn't a compelling argument compared to the massive complexities of the income tax that our Congress has imposed upon tax practitioners, the Internal Revenue Service, and small businesses.

# 10
## STOCK OPTIONS

Tax litigation is limited to disputes involving particular fact situations, but may have wide implications. Thus a court decision may send ripples among tax practitioners concerned about its implications for cases somewhat different. The trial of a litigated tax dispute tends to occur five or more years after the taxable year involved, and decisions by appellate courts even later. Thus court decisions may take a decade or longer before a relatively well-defined body of law (often confusing because different courts or judges decide similar situations differently) is developed. When tax practitioners are saying "I can't give you a firm opinion" about a planned transaction, such as a stock option given to an executive, if the class of persons involved are powerful, as executives of large corporations are, Congressional legislation is likely to be enacted quickly.

The Supreme Court opinion in **Comm v. Smith**, 324 U.S. 177 (1945) established that a stock option given to an employee could result in ordinary income. However, the opinion left the timing question uncertain. Was the amount of income to be determined (1) when the option was granted, (2) when notice of exercise was given, (3) when the stock was received, (4) when the stock was sold or (5) when the sales proceeds were received? Lobbyists argued that tax rates (91 percent was the top rate then) were so high that it was difficult adequately to motivate executives. Congress in 1950 (Democrat majorities in both the House and the Senate) enacted a provision that permitted a stock option to be granted and, if the option was exercised (at a price much below the then market value) after holding the stock for six months and one day, sold for a capital gain and taxed at a maximum rate of 25 percent.

One of our ideals is equal treatment under the law. The 1950 stock option rules gave no relief from high tax rates to high income actors, lawyers, doctors, and accountants, authors, athletes, sales personnel, stockbrokers, advertising account managers, and so on. The 1950 stock option rules favord only top management of large corporations. This was an unprincipled action by Congress.

Stock options now are subject to restrictions that were not in place when the rules were first enacted in 1950, but still exist as incentive stock options (see Sec. 422, I.R.C.). This is unjust.

The stock option rules also placed the presidents of corporations in a conflict of interest. While supposedly subject to a fiduciary duty to operate the corporation for the benefit of the shareholder, it was in the executive's personal interest to show apparent earnings growth to get the stock price up and keep it up for at least six months so they could sell and realize their income at capital gains rates. This could be done by certain accounting practices and elections. Probably the major manipulation came by not electing LIFO (Last In, First Out) inventory and continuing to use FIFO (First In, First Out).

LIFO, by matching the current cost of purchases against current sales prices, avoids showing inflationary increases in costs of inventory as income. Here is a simple example: Assume a furniture dealer buys a chair in a highly inflationary period for $150. He marks it up to $200. Later he sells it for $200, but by that time the same chair costs $200 to buy from the factory. FIFO accounting says he has a $50 profit. But he really does not have a profit, because it will cost $200 to replace the chair—and the merchant must replace inventory to say in business. Thus the FIFO "profit" is illusory in two ways: (1) replacement cost offsets the "paper" profit; and (2) to the extent other prices have risen along with furniture there has been no increase in the purchasing power of the merchant.

This example reflects a high rate of inflation, such as that under Jimmy Carter. The same principles apply, however, when inflation is at a lower rate, such as 3 percent to 6 percent annually. The chief executives were doubtlessly informed and probably intelligent enough to realize that the long-term trend would be inflation. Most large corporations, however, elected to continue FIFO despite the fact that it shows illusory income, and that income taxes had to be paid on that illusory income.

It seems inexplicable that executives would want FIFO continued for their corporation, until we realize that the illusory income drove up stock prices, enabling those executives to realize large sums at capital gains rates from stock options. The stockholders were harmed in two ways: (1) payment of excessive income tax (as compared to that payable under LIFO); (2) and dilution of their equity by issuance of stock to those executives. Furthermore, there was no deduction for the "stock" compensation to those executives. But stockholders routinely approved such stock options. A possible explanation of the approval is that our income tax is so unpopular that those who understood were glad to see others get a break from the income tax, even though it cost them.

The incentive for management to look for short-term gains, even to the detriment of long-term prospects, also was stimulated by favorable treatment of stock options. Many commentators have noted the fixation of the management of U.S. corporations on the short term, in contrast to the Japanese concern for the long term. It may be that people in middle management during the heyday of the stock options (and now in top management) developed their short-term outlook from the actions of top management at that time. They also learned stockholders could be taken for huge compensation to the top executives. This is done by management cooperating with the directors for substantial benefits for outside board members.

Some may argue that the increased stock prices contributed to confidence and economic prosperity. There is some truth to this. But can prosperity based on illusory profits and the resultant inflated stock prices continue indefinitely? One of the problems from inflation is that one reading reported income of corporations in the financial news cannot be sure how close the reports are to reality. So far, we have not put into effect accounting practices to reflect clearly income in periods of inflation.

An example of a failure of financial statements to reflect reality is that balance sheets did not have to reflect the liability to retirees and their dependents to pay for medical care if a corporation has incurred such a liability. A rule changing this became effective January 1, 1993. The net worth of many corporations dropped when this accounting rule became effective. But if the liability wasn't put on the corporation's balance sheet previously, the liability was still there, wasn't it? Were the boards of directors and top management being honest in their representations through published accounting statements? Are other questionable accounting practices now being used to keep stock prices up?

# 11
## TAX SHELTERS

A report prepared by the Treasury Department before the end of the Johnson administration and released just before the inauguration of President Nixon revealed that many individuals with substantial adjusted gross incomes paid no income taxes. (Adjusted gross income comes close to income in the economic sense, while taxable income may have little relationship to economic income.) While this revelation came as no surprise to tax experts, it resulted in a public reaction followed by the passage of the 1969 Tax Reform Act.

Previously, persons with large incomes had been able to avoid paying income tax through legitimate tax shelter principles. A tax shelter, as I use the term, means an investment that shows a loss for income tax purposes. This loss could be deducted, "sheltering" income from other sources such as salary, professional income, or taxable interest and dividends. Such losses for tax purpose are mostly artificial losses resulting from favorable tax provisions, not true economic losses.

Investments in real-estate developments illustrate how this worked. Congress enacted provisions for accelerated depreciation (more depreciation in early years and less depreciation in later years) to stimulate the economy. In an inflation context, and especially in a rapidly growing area, values of improved real estate were actually increasing rather than decreasing with the passage of time. The interest on mortgage indebtedness on commercial property was deductible, and the tax benefit was enhanced by what was called leverage. If 95 percent of the costs of buying the land and building an office building could be borrowed by the syndicate, investors put up only 5 percent of the costs. But they could deduct 100 percent of the interest and depreciation, even though they had no risk beyond the 5 percent of the costs they had invested.

The investors were typically limited partners. Limited partners can only deduct partnership losses to the amount of their basis. Basis included their pro rata share of mortgage indebtedness, not only the cash paid. As a result, many limited partners took deductions for tax "losses" several times larger than their actual investments. These deductions were used to shelter other income nominally taxed at rates up to 77 percent.

The situation revealed by the 1969 report (Democratic Party majorities in both the House and Senate) reflects adversely on the Congress. Congress should have been aware of the situation, which called for action to end the use of tax shelters. Congress did enact some half-hearted provisions, such as the alternative minimum tax, which added enormously to the complexity of the income tax. This is typical of Congressional compromises, which have added to the overwhelming complexity of our income tax. Principled action could have been simple and put an end to that tax abuse.

The result of various indebtedness to special interests is complicated compromise as provisions are added to gain the needed votes to obtain a majority of the committee. This involves complicated negotiation. A member who would vote for straight, simple and principled action may defect as exceptions are added. In the end, senators or representatives may demand an exception for a special interest in their state or district, before they will vote for the final version.

As the popularity of tax shelters increased, unscrupulous promoters joined lawyers, accountants, securities dealers, insurance people, trust officers, and so on, in marketing tax shelters. Often tax shelters were fraudulent, both upon the investors and the Internal Revenue Service. Congress enacted provision after provision dealing gradually with the tax shelter problems. The Service emphasized audits of tax shelters, and a vast amount of litigation ensued.

Real estate (realtors have one of the most effective lobbying apparatuses) was exempt from most of the restrictions placed piece meal on tax shelters. After 1984, real estate became virtually the only area left for "legal" tax shelters. The result was to funnel vast amounts of funds into real estate construction, and over-building resulted in many cities. Savings and loan associations loaned much of the funds for the leverage.

Then in 1986 Congress acted decisively to end tax shelters. The rule adopted was that a taxpayer could not deduct a loss from a passive activity against income from other sources, such as salary, professional income, dividends, and interest. This rule even applied retroactively to existing tax shelters, legal when started! A simple concept, but a simple concept may result in an unbelievably complex law, and the passive activity loss regulations are very long (144 pages in CCH ***Standard Federal Tax Reporter*** ) and very difficult to understand.

The passive activity rules affected the improved real estate market in two ways. First, it stopped the flow of tax shelter money into new real estate construction. Second, it drastically reduced the resale market for office buildings, apartment projects, shopping centers, and so on. After a real estate tax shelter had operated for a few years, the depreciation deductions dropped (accelerated depreciation is higher in early years and lower in later years); interest deductions also dropped, as some principal was repaid. The shelter could start showing a tax profit instead of a loss. Cash could be needed for debt retirement and not be available to distribute to investors. To avoid these situations the improved real estate would be sold (the gain would be a capital gain) to a new tax shelter, which could start fresh with accelerated depreciation and leveraged interest deductions. This resale market disappeared once tax shelters were curbed in 1986. One of the consequences was large losses to savings and loan associations which had loaned money for the tax shelters, which, incidentally, helped bring about overbuilding in many cities.

If Congress had taken principled, simple action in 1969 to end tax shelters, the savings and loan bail-out might not have been necessary. (Congress also blundered by raising the insured amount to $100,000.) Also, tens of thousands of tax-shelter investors would have been spared real losses of money, plus tax deficiencies, penalties, interest, and the costs of audit and litigation. Most litigation was lost by investors because the visions of paying little income tax blinded them to economic reality. Many believed the statements of con men selling tax shelters. The courts held that where there was no realistic profit motive, paper losses could not be deducted.

Professor Jeffrey Pennell of the Emory University Law faculty speaking at an Advanced Estate Planning Institute sponsored by the American Law Institute/American Bar Association at the University of Wisconsin in June, 1992 said that early in recent Congresses legislation would be introduced to change adversely some income tax advantages of life insurance; then after contributions came in from the life insurance industry, the legislation would quietly die the next year. So in effect members of the Ways and Means Committee and the Senate Finance Committee are in a position not merely to solicit contributions, but also to extort contributions.

# 12
# 1986 *TAX REFORM ACT* TRANSITION RULES

The transition rules in the 1986 Tax Reform Act (TRA) to a large degree grew out of the rules it contained to curb tax shelters. As the 1986 TRA made its way through Congress, some persons involved in real estate tax shelters became aware of plans to curb such shelters. The proposed rules would affect such shelters adversely. Intense lobbying occurred to exempt some tax shelters, as well as other taxpayers, from the new rules. For example, Senator Packwood, chairman of the Senate Finance Committee, received more than six million dollars in contributions in 1986. Senator Dole, majority leader and a member of the Senate Finance Committee, received more than two million dollars in contributions in 1986. Both Dole and Packwood were candidates for reelection in 1986, and certainly not all of the contributions can be attributed to the lobbying for the transition rules. But those who believe the adage, We have the best Congress money can buy, find support for their position in this 1986 lobbying.

There were more than 650 such transition rules. The revenue cost (lower revenue from not applying the new rules to some taxpayers) was $10.6 billion. However, an article in the ***Philadelphia Inquirer*** (September 27, 1986) stated that the number was actually much higher than 650. Also, that article contended that the revenue cost might be two or three times as great as the amount given by the Senate Finance Committee chairman.

These rules have been called "rifle shot transition rules." This means each transition rule was intended to benefit one specific taxpayer or tax shelter, unlike most tax legislation, which is intended to apply broadly to many taxpayers falling within some classification. The project would not be stated by name, but the description would fit only one project or one taxpayer. For example, a 1986 transition rule benefitting contributors to the athletic programs at Louisiana State University describes the univesity this way:

> mandated by a State constitution in 1876, established by a State legislature in March 1881, located in a State capital pursuant to a statewide election in September, 1881, [having a] campus formally opened on September 15, 1883, and operated under the authority of a 9-member board of regents appointed by the governor.

Similar relief was granted for the University of Texas. Why those two universities? Russell Long of Louisiana and Lloyd Bentsen of Texas were both on the Senate Finance Committee.

There were more than three hundred transition rules adopted by the conference committee on the 1986 TRA <u>that were in neither the House bill nor the Senate bill!</u> Why? Because Bob Packwood and Dan Rostenkowski agreed to them.

If Bob Dole, Bob Packwood, and Dan Rostenkowski were asked to defend these very special exemptions, their defense would be roughly as follows:

> A popular president wanted tax reform. There was sentiment in the country as a whole for tax reform. Some people were going to be hurt. We couldn't get the votes to pass the TRA without granting exemptions to various specific taxpayers as requested by various Congressmen on behalf of constituents or contributors.

That argument can be summed up as: "We did wrong for a greater good."

The rifle shot transition rules in the 1986 TRA were an unprincipled action by Congress. Principled action would have been to enact some general guidelines for who should receive relief for hardships resulting from the 1986 TRA. Then leave it up to the IRS and the courts to decide who received relief and what the relief would be. Granting transition relief in closed committee meetings gets close to the shadowy lines among contributions, bribery, gifts and extortion.

An interesting case arose out of the unprincipled action of the Congress in the 1986 TRA Transition Rules. Apache Bend Apartments didn't ask for Congressional favors; instead it sued to enjoin the special favors granted to others in similar situations. These were persons who had connections with lobbyists and Congressmen on either the House Ways and Means Committee or the Senate Finance Committee. Apache Bend Apartments lost before the 5th Circuit, *en banc* ( all judges on that court, rather than the usual three judge panel) because of lack of standing to sue. **Apache Bend Apts. v U.S. Through I.R.S.**, 987 F.2d 1174 (5th Cir., 1993). Here is the opening three sentences of the final opinion, 987 F.2d 1174, 1175:

> In the Tax Reform Act of 1986, Congress included "transition rules," which provided specified exemptions from designated provisions of the new tax laws to a very, very few specified favored taxpayers. The plaintiff taxpayers were not among the very, very favored few. They brought this suit to scotch the wheels of the greased wagon.

In the earlier opinion by a three-judge panel from the 5th Circuit, the following language appears at 964 F.2d 1556, 1567:

> The district court catalogued the many references in the legislative history to political favoritism exhibited by members of Congress. *See* 702 F.Supp. at 1287-89. For example, the Chairman of the Senate Finance Committee (Bob Packwood) confessed that
>
> > [i]t would be foolish of me to say that, on occasion, politics did not enter those judgments. If the Speaker of the House

> requested [of] the chairman of the Ways and Means Committee a transition rule, my hunch is that [he] would give it reasonably high priority in his thinking.
>
> If Senator Dole requested one of me, I would give it reasonably high priority in my thinking.

132 Cong.Rec. S13,786 (daily ed. Sept. 26, 1986) (statement of Sen. Packwood).

Another Senator "admitted using his position on the committee to obtain special treatment for his constituents." 702 F. Supp. at 1288.

> I do not mind saying to my colleagues that I have used my position on the Finance Committee to the advantage of the people of Minnesota.... I have used my position to get special rules for my people....

132 Cong.Rec. S8,221 (daily ed. June 24, 1986) (statement of Sen. Durenberger).

The three opinions in **Apache Bend Apts.** can be used by supporters of term limits. See also the dissenting opinion at 987 F.2d 1174, 1187.

Do more senior members of Congress, especially those in leadership positions or chairmen of powerful committees such as Ways and Means and Senate Finance Committee, tend to vote differently from junior members? Specifically, are they more likely to vote in support of Washington bureaucracies like the Treasury Department and the IRS?

Payne, ***Costly Returns*** (discussed in chapter 1), p. 176, did an analysis of the pro-IRS voting records of more senior and more junior members of the Senate Finance Committee on four issues. The average pro-IRS score for more senior members was

2.71; the average pro-IRS score for more junior members was 1.69. Senator Danforth (R-Mo.) scored highest with 4.0. Senator Dole (R-Kan.) and Senator Packwood (R-Ore.) at 3.0 tied for second highest, along with three other senators.

One of Dole's pro-IRS votes was on interest withholding in 1982. In a speech in Washington he said he voted for that because of a request by President Reagan. After passage there was the strong protest organized by the Savings and Loan Associations and others. Senator Dole then voted for the repeal of that withholding provision. My thesis is that Senator Dole, along with many others in Congress, votes for Treasury and the IRS, but not when he detects strong opposition and interest from the public.

Who could have stopped the unprincipled action of Congress with the 1986 TRA Transition Rules? A bi-partisan foursome, Majority Leader Dole in the Senate and Bob Packwood, chair of the Senate Finance Committee; Majority Leader Jim Wright in the House of Representatives and Dan Rostenkowski, chair of the House Ways and Means Committee. But there might not have been a 1986 TRA!

There is a book on the passage of the 1986 TRA: Birnbaum and Murray, ***Showdown at Gucci Gulch*** (Random House, New York, 1987). For a discussion of constitutional issues by a law professor, see Zelenak, "Are Rifle Shot Transition Rules and Other Ad Hoc Tax Legislation Constitutional?" 44 ***Tax Law Review*** 563 (1989).

## 13
## PERCENTAGE DEPLETION

Depletion describes what happens as minerals or other materials are extracted from the earth and the amount remaining is thereby reduced. Depletion is similar to depreciation for structures and tangible personal property; under a net income tax, the owner of a mineral deposit should be entitled to a deduction for the exhaustion of the deposit.

During World War I, Congress enacted a provision providing for depletion of oil wells based upon discovery value, not cost. This was intended to stimulate the production of oil for the war effort. A substantial increase in value occurs, when oil is discovered in sufficient quantities to be commercially worthwhile. That increase in value would be exempt from income tax through a deduction. This was called "discovery value depletion" (in contrast to "cost depletion.").

In chapter 3 on controversy-generating aspects of the income tax, the fair market value of property was mentioned as a factual issue that frequently creates disputes between the Internal Revenue Service and taxpayers. This issue arises in several areas, such as the value of property under the estate and gift tax or the value of property-in-kind received as compensation for services, for example, when a lawyer receives a tract of land as payment for services. In most areas the motivation of the taxpayer is to seek a low value, while the motive of the Service is to assert a higher value. In the case of discovery value depletion, however, the motivations were reversed.

Discovery value depletion for oil enacted during World War I did not have a time limit; that is, there was no provision for it to expire once the war was over. In fact, revenue acts were enacted every two years by the new Congress, and percentage depletion was re-enacted through the Revenue Act of 1924. Through the years, the Treasury Department and Internal Revenue became convinced that taxpayers were asserting unduly high discovery values in order to increase the amount of the deductions. The Treasury Department did a study and concluded that if discovery value was more accurately determined, it would equal a depletion allowance of 27.5 percent of the gross income from oil itself (before processing).

So, in effect, percentage depletion for oil came in as a tax reform in 1926 to curb an abuse. There is no objection to percentage depletion as a method for determining depletion, provided that when the cost is fully recovered, the deductions stop. No doubt there have been many instances where cost has been recovered hundreds of times over. This obviously is an objectionable discrimination against taxpayers who do not have percentage depletion. In effect, those in the oil industry were deducting amounts that were fictitious, not actual costs.

For many years percentage depletion in the oil industry was denounced in various publications. Often I would ask those who expressed opposition to the percentage depletion why they felt it was objectionable. With an occasional exception for a person who was teaching tax or some related subject such as accounting, those who thought percentage depletion was objectionable did not realize precisely what was discriminatory (that it is unrelated to cost) against other taxpayers. This helped convince me that it is very difficult to expose discriminatory and objectionable aspects of the income tax law, even to intelligent people.

After the 1926 provision eliminating discovery depletion and replacing it with 27.5 percent of gross income depletion for oil wells, percentage depletion gradually spread to other industries extracting minerals. The Congressmen who understood the bonanza that the oil-producing regions were receiving wanted their constituents to be in on the favorable—but unjustified—treatment. Percentage depletion spread to almost every conceivable extractive industry. Once that happened, I assumed that percentage depletion was invulnerable to repeal. An overwhelming majority of Congressional districts and states would have at least some extractive industry that would be pressuring Congressmen and senators not to take away the bonanza.

Congress did eventually place a ceiling on the percentage depletion; it could not exceed 50 percent of net income from the property. However, in the case of the oil industry, percentage depletion was only part of the favorable tax treatment. There was recognized, long ago, a deduction for what is called "intangible drilling expense." This is the cost of putting the hole in the ground. If the well were a dry hole, normal accounting practice would be to write off the full cost as a loss. Under normal accounting treatment, the cost of a successful well would be capitalized and become part of the base for cost depletion. However, the income tax regulations gave taxpayers a choice. They could deduct the full amount of their intangible drilling expense, or they could add it to the base for cost depletion. Percentage depletion was always higher, so naturally the choice was to expense the intangible drilling expense.

In the 1940s there was concern that the Treasury Department might change the regulation and take away the election to deduct intangible drilling expenses. In 1945 Congress (Democratic majorities in both the House and the Senate) adopted a joint resolution prohibiting the Treasury Department from changing the regulation.

The combination of percentage depletion and the right to elect to deduct intangible drilling expense, even when a producing well was achieved, meant that the oil and gas industry probably had the most favorable tax treatment of any industry in the country. A large oil company could do enough drilling to produce intangible drilling expense sufficient to eliminate the 50 percent of net income that could not be taken under the ceiling on percentage depletion. In effect, a large oil company could pay virtually no income tax, and there were many instances when this in fact did happen.

When the Arab embargo of oil shipments to the United States occurred in the early 1970s, shortages of gasoline developed. Many citizens were exasperated by long lines at gasoline pumps. Stations might not have gasoline at any given time. This resentment resulted in percentage depletion for the oil and gas industry being eliminated for large producers, although it still continues for small producers and for royalty owners.

The resentment of the public, however, did not extend to the other extractive industries, in which percentage depletion still continues. While the election to deduct intangible drilling expense still exists, a portion of intangible drilling expenses and the excess of percentage depletion over cost depletion are both items entering into the computation of the alternative minimum tax. The rate of taxation on corporations for preference items is lower than the normal corporate income tax. So the percentage depletion deduction allowed to the various extractive industries other than oil and gas still is objectionable, because it is not an actual cost.

That percentage depletion has persisted for almost seventy years—and in fact has expanded from oil to other extractive industries—is an illustration of the capacity of Congress to use the income tax in unprincipled ways.

# 14
## CHARITABLE DEFERRED GIVING

A spouse in a childless marriage might decide to have a will placing property in trust with income to be paid to the surviving spouse for life and then the trust property to go to a charity (the legal term is a "remainder" after the life estate). Our society long has recognized the good done by charities. The present value of that charitable remainder (discounted for the life expectancy of the surviving spouse at an interest rate prescribed by regulation) of that charitable remainder would not be subject to estate tax. Income tax could also be saved by creating the trust while the donor was alive. Such a trust could provide income to the donor for life, then, if the spouse survived, to the spouse for life, and then to the charity.

Until 1969 this area of tax law was well established. Then the Treasury Department created a rigid, complicated scheme that Congress enacted into law, turning an area of law working reasonably well into a quagmire.

After 1969 (Democratic Party majorities in both the House and Senate) it became clear that the Congress often didn't realize the consequences of what it was doing in the tax area. In the same 1969 Act, it unknowingly enacted the marriage penalty.

The argument the Treasury Department used for the new rules on "charitable remainder" trusts was this: There were instances where trustees made risky investments to yield high income, thereby risking that the charity would get nothing. State laws already in place kept such abuses minimial. The prudent investor rule (in effect in all states) only permits trustees to make investments

> "which men of prudence, discretion and intelligence [would make] in the management of their own affairs, not in regard to speculation, but in regard to the permanent disposition of their funds, considering the probable income, as well as the probable safety of their capital."

In short, if a trustee loses the property from risky investments, the charity can sue and the trustee has to make the loss good. While there occasionally may be a "happy-go-lucky" family member as trustee, that is atypical. Trustees act carefully and fear surcharges (the legal term for a trustee paying for some improper action). A high percentage are financially responsible—banks and, increasingly in recent years, stock brokerage firms—and they routinely get advice from competent attorneys.

The law of trusts had evolved over four centuries and by 1969 was well established. Typically lawyers working in that area understood the law, an important part of which was principal and income acts. These set out the fiduciary duties of a trustee to act fairly as to both the income beneficiaries and the remainder interest after the death of the last income beneficiary.

In effect, Congress supplanted this well-settled body of law with a rigid scheme written and passed by Congressmen blissfully ignorant of the harm they were doing. The principal concept of the new legislation was that to qualify for a deduction under the income tax, gift tax, and the estate tax, the amount paid the spouse or some relative prior to the charity receiving the property had to take one of two forms. It could be either:

> **An annuity**—that is, a sum certain paid not less frequently than annually
>
> or
>
> **A unitrust**—that is, a fixed percentage of the trust assets valued annually, paid not less frequently than annually.

The provision was a page and a half in the I.R.C. (Internal Revenue Code) (CCH printing) and fifty-seven pages in the regulations (CCH printing).

What happened here, and has occurred over and over again, is that some remote possibility of tax avoidance is thought up by the Treasury, and obtuse language is proposed and enacted to require an express prohibition of that remote possibility in the governing instrument. Then some person, not learned in this monstrosity, drafts an instrument that does explicitly preclude that remote possibility. He or shee then finds a revenue agent saying "Gotcha! You owe lots of tax!" The rich, with access to the best lawyers and accountants, can cope; the larger businesses can cope. The only salvation for others is that the IRS can't cope with the income tax as it now exists. That saves the rest of the country from what could be disaster if the income tax were 100 percent enforced.

The Internal Revenue Service unfortunately took a hyper-critical approach to these deferred gifts to charity. It imposed tax deficiencies for trivial deviations from the words in the Internal Revenue Code. Generally the law applies a *de minimis* doctrine—"the law does not care for, or take notice of, very small or trifling matters." But Internal Revenue Service did care about such matters under the 1969 Act. If an honest, well-intentioned donor, represented by a well-intentioned, competent lawyer (but not a specialist in deferred charitable giving) attempted to make a deferred gift to charity, the IRS might be able to find some trivial, technical reason to disallow any income tax deduction. Even worse, the IRS might impose either a gift tax or estate tax on the value going to charity. This could happen even though a substantial value was going to charity, and there was not the slightest evidence of any intention to manipulate the charity out of its rights.

When Congress enacts stupid legislation, and constituents begin to suffer the consequences, the members hear from the sufferers. Congress reacted by enacting and annually extending authority to reform these trusts and thereby still qualify for a deduction. Then, by legislation, it created a permanent (no time limit) right to reform trusts making deferred gifts to charity. So this situation now is not as bad as it once was. But as long as we have an income tax, the country is at risk. The potential is always there for Treasury Department officials, who do not understand what they are doing to the country by heaping complexities on top of complexities, to have a subservient Congress enact their proposals.

There are two cases, in which I as an attorney was personally involved, which are summarized below to show how bad the situation on these charitable remainder gifts was for about fifteen years.

In one case, there was a valid existing charitable remainder trust for the Indiana University Foundation. It was a substantial trust in which the donor was receiving an annuity for his life before the Foundation received the trust property. The trust property was several hundreds of thousands of dollars in value. His financial affairs had improved, and he wanted to turn one-half of the trust property over to the Foundation immediately and reduce his annuity by one half. I was asked for my opinion. I could not find an exact precedent. Nonetheless, for an intelligent, fair-minded person who understands the law, the proper result should be obvious: There is an additional income tax deduction for the actuarial value of the one-half of the lifetime annuity that the donor was surrendering. But one cannot count on consistently dealing with intelligent, fair-minded IRS personnel, so I advised asking for an advance ruling from IRS.

The Service ruled that this partial release would be subject to the gift tax. and there would be no income tax deduction. The principal reason appeared to be that the annuity would no longer be an "amount certain"—that is, the annuity payment would not be the same as the original annuity payment when the annuity trust was first established. This reasoning ignored the fact that the annuity was for an amount certain *before* the partial release and would be for an amount certain (although a different and lower amount) *after* the partial release of a corresponding portion of the principal. Nothing in the statute said or implied that the annuity could not be reduced proportionately to a release of a portion of the trust property outright to the charity.

Naturally, the donor didn't want to engage in litigation to contest the ruling, and the charity lost what would have been a present, completely received gift in place of a portion of a deferred gift. Thus the Service warped legislation intended to assure that a charity would receive its remainder to prevent its receiving even more—present possessory ownership.

In the other case, a woman left a life estate in farmland and a residence to her elderly sister. The property was then to go 90 percent to charity and 10 percent to a relative who was a Christian minister. But it went to him as an individual, so it was not a charitable gift to the minister. Congress had made an exception to the 1969 provisions on charitable remainder trusts for life estates in farmland and residences. These did not have to be in the form of an annuity, because there was no opportunity to manipulate income in those situations.

By the time the estate tax return was audited and was in controversy, the elderly sister had died. Thus it had become a certainty that charity would get its 90 percent. Nevertheless, the estate tax deduction was disallowed. The reason was an illogical published ruling. That ruling said that 100 percent of the remainder had to go to charity after a life estate in farmland or a residence for there to be a deduction. (When in doubt, rule against the taxpayer.) When there is a fixed percentage to go to charity after a life estate in a farm or a residence, there is no opportunity for manipulation. That published ruling was indefensible by intelligent argument.

I was employed to represent the estate. The appeals officer in Indianapolis was very sympathetic when I had a conference with him. He agreed that the published ruling was wrong. But his hands were tied since it was a published ruling from the national office that was a precedent, not distinguishable.

The estate paid the additional tax. We then filed a claim for refund with IRS, followed by a suit for refund in Federal District Court for the Northern District of Indiana. Now I was dealing with an attorney from the Tax Division of the Department of Justice. He was intelligent and agreed with my position. He persuaded his superiors. A full refund of all additional tax plus interest was received. The IRS had promised to revoke the prior published ruling, and that was done about eighteen months later.

Thomas M. McGlasson, an attorney practicing in Bloomington, remembers a conversation which included myself, him, and some others at a tax conference in Washington, D.C., in March 1970. At that time, I expressed my opinion that the new rules on charitable deferred giving would cause much trouble. If we are to keep the income tax, a consulting group of people, with experience out in the field handling tax disputes, should be established to advise Congress about Treasury Department proposals. Congress would do better listening to such a group than listening to Treasury and their Congressional staffs in Washington, D.C.

While I have a generally favorable opinion of the top echelon personnel in the national IRS and the Treasury Department, there is one serious problem. There are few, if any, who have had day-to-day experience in handling and litigating income tax disputes. Neither they nor the Congressmen who listen to their legislative proposals understand the problems some of these proposals will create for small businesses, self-employed persons, and almost everyone away from the large cities. The longer someone is in Congress, the more likely the or she is to believe in and rely upon advice from the Treasury Department and the IRS.

Artificial schemes, that is, those not evolved from experience, should be suspect. The excess profits taxes, the first generation skipping tax (probably also the second generation skipping tax), the rules on deferred charitable giving, the delegation of authority to develop regulations on debt-equity issues, are examples of such schemes. There is a tendency for Washington to impose schemes which are largely beyond the level of intelligence, knowledge, and judgment of the people assigned to administer the income tax legislation and regulations.

## 15
## THE MARRIAGE PENALTY

The marriage penalty, created in the 1969 Act (Democratic Party majorities in both the House and Senate) illustrates (1) that Congress doesn't know what it is doing in the income tax area and (2) how difficult it is for a broad group of people discriminated against under the income tax by Congress, to be alerted to the existence of that discrimination and persuaded to achieve retribution by defeating incumbent Congressmen. Congress in 1969 lowered rates for single taxpayers.

Did Congress in 1969 create the marriage penalty, knowingly as a conscious major policy decision? Of course not. As was said by the court in **Druker v. Comm.**, 697 F.2d 46, 50 (2d Cir. 1982)

> "It would be altogether absurd to suppose that Congress had any invidious intent to discourage or penalize marriage—an estate enjoyed by the vast majority of its members."

Congress simply did not notice that it was taxing millions of married persons (where both have income) more heavily than if they were living together unmarried.

The marriage penalty was not recognized in the 1969 reports of the Ways and Means Commerce or of the Senate Finance Committee. There was not a great debate followed by the news media with married persons and single persons eagerly contacting their Congressman. True the Staff of the Joint Committee on Taxation issued a report months after the 1969 Act became effective acknowledging the existence of the marriage penalty. But this suggests the question, "Who is running the shop, the staff or the Congressmen?"

So what is this marriage penalty?

If only one of the spouses has income, and the other no income, under current rate tables there is an income tax advantage from being married (some authors call it a tax bonus). This is also true if one spouse has a small income relative to the income of the other spouse. The penalty against marriage is greatest when the incomes of the spouses are equal. The so-called tax bonus has a historical explanation. In 1948 when two "earner" families were not common, there was a tax advantage to residents of community property states where the income was automatically split by state law. The 1948 joint return and split income provision was justified to eliminate that discrimination.

To illustrate the current discrimination against married persons with equal incomes, I assume the simplest case, use of a standard deduction and personal exemptions and no other feature affecting tax liability, such as dependents. I use the 1994 income tax tables and rates:

| Total Adjusted Gross Income | Income Tax Liability (Married) | Income Tax Liability (Living together Unmarried) | Marriage Penalty |
|---|---|---|---|
| $ 53,100 ($26,550 each) | $ 6,771.00 | $ 6,089.00 | $ 673.00 |
| $117,800 ($58,900 each) | $ 25,133.00 | $ 23,584.00 | $ 1,549.00 |
| $237,500 ($118,800 each) | $ 63,372.50 | $ 60,561.00 | $ 2,811.50 |
| $307,600 ($153,800 each) | $ 93,659.10 | $ 83,515.00 | $10,144.10 |
| $507,600 ($253,800 each) | $177,194.10 | $157,515.00 | $19,679.10 |

The marriage penalty can operate upon persons with modest incomes entitled to earned income credits. Assume a single man and a single woman each having an adjusted gross income of $8,425 (all earned income). Two children live with each. In 1994, unmarried, each pays no income tax and receives a refund of $2,528.00 under the earned income credit. If they had married they still would have paid no income tax but would have received a refund of only $1,489.00. The total penalty is $3,567.00 (2x $2,528.00 minus $1,489.00).

The penalty also can affect the elderly receiving social security benefits. Assume a man and a woman, each unmarried, living with one dependent grandchild , and having an adjusted gross income of $19,000 and receiving $12,000 a year in social security benefits based on their own earnings. Using the standard deduction, each would pay $1,136 income tax. If they marry and use the standard deduction, their income tax is $4,721. The marriage penalty is $2,449 ($4,721.00 less twice $1,136.)

Congress in 1981 enacted a provision for a deduction for two-earner married couples (10 percent of the lower of $30,000 or the earned income of the one with lowest earnings). This gave some relief from the marriage penalty , but it was repealed by the 1986 Act. A modification of the standard deduction in the 1986 Act did result in a slight reduction in the marriage penalty for those who do not itemize deductions. After the 1986 Act the standard deduction in 1987 was $3,760 for married persons and $2,540 for single persons. After the 1986 Act was fully effective in 1988, the amounts were respectively $5,000 for married persons , and $3,000 for single persons. (For 1994 the standard deduction was $6,350 for married filing jointly and $3,800 for a single person.) When Congress repealed the two-earner deduction in 1986, the reasoning was that with lower tax rates the marriage penalty should be tolerable. Tax rates were lowered both for married and unmarried persons; therefore, it is proper to leave the marriage penalty as a permanent feature of the income tax! With reasoning like that coming from the Congress one fears for the future of the Republic.

One aspect of the marriage penalty may offer hope. The people who realize that the income tax is fatally flawed, and constantly more do, are a minority of the voters (primarily the self-employed and small businessmen). But most of the victims of the marriage penalty, as well as potential victims (people who may marry, with both having salaries or incomes approximately equal in amount), are subject only to withholding; they don't learn the relentless lesson of managing cash flow to pay estimated tax, as well as employment taxes, faced by small businessmen. People concerned about family values, ministers, some media people, service club members (especially program schedulers) and so on, should publicize this marriage penalty. Why not urge married people to write to their Congressmen, saying, "No vote for an incumbent until the marriage penalty is gone." Hopefully many citizens will come to realize that the income tax is dangerous in the hands of a Congress that doesn't know what it is doing. They should support a repeal of the income tax and the substitution of some revenue scheme that does not involve so many problems.

Besides the marriage penalty Congress hurt the family by failing to increase the amount of the personal exemption and the dependency deduction (also the width of the rate brackets) to keep pace with inflation over the period from 1945 to 1981. In 1981 President Reagan obtained indexing of the personal exemption and the dependency deduction for inflation, as well as bracket width. If the $500 dependency deduction in 1945 had been indexed for inflation continuously since then, it would be at least $4,000 in 1994. Since it actually is $2,450, multiply your number of exemptions and dependency deductions by $1,550 to obtain some idea of the extra tax you are paying courtesy of the grow-the-government party. And remember that when that party makes an effort to abolish indexing for inflation.

# 16
## THE 1993 CLINTON TAX BILL

There are several aspects of the 1993 Clinton Tax Bill (Democratic Party majorities in both the House and Senate) that merit criticism. It increases complexity. It continues the pattern of constant change, which impairs the ability of individuals and businesses to plan ahead on the assumption that the tax laws will stay the same. The bill was passed so narrowly that it would have failed if a single vote had been lost to Clinton in either the House or Senate. We saw the spectacle of Clinton using promises of (or threats to) use of his powers and funds available to him to either pressure for or buy the votes of reluctant members of his party. Many of them were retired in 1994; retiring Clinton in 1996 and the rest of those who voted for the 1993 Clinton Tax Bill will be a step in the right direction.

The argument for the Reagan 1986 Tax Reform Act was to reduce the rates, to have fewer brackets, thus reducing motivation for shifting income to persons in lower brackets, and to close "loopholes." The history of high tax rates (as high as 91 percent, 87 percent, 77 percent, 70 percent, 50 percent) Shows that, when high "nominal" rates existed, there were standard tax planning techniques available, so that the average effective tax rates on persons with higher incomes rarely exceeded about 40 percent. It's a fair statement that Congress never really believed in those high rates. True, Sergeant York, Joe Louis, and Willie Nelson could get caught by the highest effective rates.

After 1986, there was a zero rate for persons with low incomes, combined with a refundable earned income credit (huge numbers of persons entitled to this refund never get it because they don't file returns, or anyone filing a return for them doesn't understand the credit), a 15% bracket and a 28% bracket. That strikes me as a significant graduated and simple rate structure, and numerous loopholes were closed.

Clinton, George Mitchell (D-Maine), Richard Gephardt (D-Missouri), and others say the new 36 percent and 39.6 percent brackets are fair, and most people probably agree with the general concept that persons with higher incomes should pay more tax. However, two scholars have questioned the arguments for a progressive rate structure, Blum and Klaven, "The Uneasy Case For Progressive Taxation, (19 ***U.Ch.L.Rev***. 417 [1952]). But to believe that one can prove by rigorous logic that a rate of x% for y income is "fair" is similar to believing in the tooth fairy. In reality, it is a political decision: We won't lose many votes by a 39.6 percent rate since only a small percentage are in the top brackets, and we can spread the tax money from them around to buy the votes of persons with lower incomes or no income, while preaching being humanitarian. But not many people in the 39.6 percent bracket think it is fair.

The experience of the last 15 years shows that states with the highest taxes, workmen's compensation, burdensome regulations, and so forth have poorer economic performance than states with lower taxes and less burdensome regulations. We live in a global economy, and the same thing is happening to our whole country that has happened to such states as New York and California. It is frightening, but not surprising, to read in ***Fortune*** that the president of Alcoa had a study made of the feasibility of moving the place of incorporation outside the United States because of the burdensome income tax situation, but was deterred from doing so by $500 million of tax exit penalties. Nonetheless, individuals can still move without penalty and take their capital with them. Since the United States purports to tax citizens on worldwide income, in order legally to stop paying U.S. income tax, such expatriates have to renounce U.S. citizenship. Expatriation has increased since the 1993 Clinton Tax Act, and at least one wealthy person made news by taking Belizean citizenship in place of U.S. citizenship. There are many tax haven countries with secrecy laws. How much U.S. capital has gone to tax havens beyond the reach of 1099s, and with income not reported by U.S. citizens, is unknowable. It is surely more extensive in 1995 than in 1992. While renouncing U.S. citizenship can give instant relief from U.S. income tax, there is a provision that the federal estate tax (top 55 percent rate) will apply for a ten-year period if estate tax avoidance was a motive for expatriation. I doubt that any tax will be collected under that provision unless the person happens directly to own real estate in the United States under his or her own name when death occurs.

***Forbes*** (November 21, 1994) published an article entitled "TheNew Refugees" ("As their tax burdens grow, many affluent Americans are abandoning their citizenship"):

> "In 1981 Ronald Reagan lowered taxes. The following year not a single American gave up his citizenship. In 1993 the expa triate community grew by 306 names." [The actual number for 1993 was 697; the number for 1994 was 858.](p. 131)

Michael Kinsley in ***Time*** magazine (November 28, 1994) revived the sixties' "Love It or Leave It" slogan to castigate these rich "yacht people" for leaving the United States. But let's try to assume for a moment the viewpoint of the wealthy person. In states with higher income tax rates, they will pay more than 50 percent of their income in combined federal and state income taxes. They also face combined federal estate taxes (55 percent) and state death taxes (which vary but are up toas high as 70 percent). In most tax havens, they can avoid both income and estate taxes.

Many believe that the quality of our federal government is declining. Crime is increasing, and cultural indices are declining.

Poor or poorly educated women are paid cash for having illegitimate children. Surely much crime results from such unwise action. Who wants to pay high taxes to such a government?

American citizens are free to leave the country and renounce their citizenship. That it is happening is not a favorable omen. But even worse are trends toward inferior public schools, with many second-rate and/or unconcerned teachers; the growth of the federal government, with a concomitant decrease in our freedoms; and ever-increasing waste.

When are the tax rates too high? If combined federal and state income taxes and combined federal and state death taxes are causing wealthy people to flee the country, the rates are too high.

In February 1995 the Clinton administration proposed a 35 percent tax on the amount of appreciation in value of assets of persons renouncing their U.S. citizenship. A person planning to renounce citizenship for tax reasons would be unlikely to pay this 35 percent tax voluntarily. Once the assets are titled in a secret trust or bank account in a tax haven country, the United States is in no position to collect such a tax. True, the federal government can refuse to recognize the renunciation of citizenship, but once the people have acquired citizenship in another country,they are not likely to pay income tax to the United States on their worldwide income.

Perhaps the most appalling single provision in the 1993 Clinton Tax Act is the rate table for the taxable income of estates and trusts:

| Taxable Income | Taxable Rate |
|---|---|
| $0 - $1,500 | 15% |
| $1,500 - $3,500 | 28% |
| $3,500 - $5,500 | 31% |
| $5,500 - $7,500 | 36% |
| Over $7,500 | 39.6% |

It should be noted that the 1990 Bush-Mitchell-Gephardt Tax Act enacted the first "compressed" tax rates for estates and trusts:

| Taxable Income | Taxable Rate |
|---|---|
| Under $3,750 | 15% |
| $3,750 - $11,250 | 28% |
| Over $11,250 | 31% |

That rate table also is appalling, only less appalling in degree.

Historically the rate table for trusts and estates has mostly been the same as (or close to) for individuals. Since there is a deduction for distributions, a trust or estate distributing all income will not pay any income tax, but the tax will be paid by the distributees.

But the function of a decedent's estate is to gather and hold assets (with some exceptions, such as an allowance for a surviving spouse) until debts and tax liabilities are ascertained and satisfied, before making distributions to those benefitting under the will (or by state laws providing for inheritance from persons without wills). Indeed, any executor who distributes assets and then has insufficient assets left to pay federal tax liabilities can be personally liable for such unpaid taxes. Also, people rarely die for tax planning purposes. As Franklin said, Death and taxes are always with us. (Why pair death and taxes - we only die once?) Surely these extraordinarily high rates should not apply to estates for at least the normal period of administration of an estate.

The trend toward increased retroactivity in tax legislation is a sign that many Congressmen don't really care what they do to taxpayers in obscure provisions that only tax practitioners understand. They don't expect to lose elections because of such things, which are difficult to explain to the general public.

The retroactivity of tax rate changes to January 1, 1993, twenty days before Clinton was inaugurated, is widely known. A much more objectionable retroactivity is that these high estate and trust income tax rates apply to irrevocable trusts created even before the 1990 legislation was enacted. Was any Congressman asking if it is fair to apply these higher rates to existing trusts containing provisions for mandatory accumulation of income?

If Bob Dole (on the Senate Finance Committee) wasn't asking that question in either 1990 or 1993, does he deserve the Republican nomination for President? He has yet another retroactive provision on his record. He was both majority leader and on the Senate Finance Committee in 1986 when deductions for tax shetler investmentss—legal when made earlier—were made nondeductible for future years. Many persons suffered large losses from this move.

The 1993 Clinton Tax Act taxes 85 percent of Social Security benefits, starting at $34,000 (single) and $44,000 (married) of income, as well as continuing a 50 percent tax rate on Social Security benefits starting at $25,000 (single) and $32,000 (married) of income. Isn't that actually a cut in Social Security benefits for middle class taxpayers? Why was it made effective for 1994, and not 1993? Could it be so that those paying the extra tax on April 15, 1995 would not feel the pain until after the 1994 elections? And with the new 85 percent tax on Social Security Benefits persons who have retirement income from savings are penalized. Basically, there is a penalty for having been prudent and saved for additional retirement income besides Social Security.

A more fundamental issue about this middle-class Social Security tax is the right to recover costs free of tax under a net income tax. The costs were (1) the tax on the employee which could not be deducted, and (2) an indirect decrease in earnings resulting from the matching payroll tax on the employer. The employer tax reduces funds which otherwise could have gone into direct compensation of employees. Since the Social Security taxes were not deductible, the effective income tax rate on employees' available income during their working life were higher than the stated income tax rates.

While the tax is called FICA (Federal Insurance Contributions Act), benefits are not in proportion to taxes paid. For instance, a person paying three times as much Social Security tax will not receive three times as much in benefits; it might only be one-and-one-half times as much. So there is discrimination against middle-class Social Security recipients in two ways: (1) the level of benefits, and (2) a penalty for saving and having other income.

If the costs of retired middle-class social security recipients were adjusted for inflation, as they should be (and for lost income they could have had on the amounts taken), many of those paying tax on 85 percent of their benefits will never recover their costs (adjusted for tax paid, lost income and inflation) free of tax by the 15 percent not taxed. That is an injustice under a net income tax.

If the original decision had been to permit the employee to deduct Social Security taxes but pay income tax on benefits, that would have been logical. But to deny a deduction <u>and</u> tax benefits, is an illustration that the Congress doesn't know or care about what it is doing in the income tax area.

To some extent the victims of this unjust tax on Social Security benefits can plan to minimize the harm done to them. They can invest in growth, low-yield investments to lower income, and then sell assets for living expenses as needed. Only the sales price in excess of cost is income. They can buy commercial annuities; only a small part of the receipts is income, for there is a provision for recovering cost free of income tax. Or they can move to a country such as Mexico where funds will go farther. However, if savings are invested in income sources in Mexico, the law says they must pay U.S. income tax as a citizen even if no 1099s (information returns by payors of interest, dividends, filed by Social Security numbers) are filed for the payees. Some will seek to avoid this injustice by transferring income-producing assets to children, who promise to return the income to their parents. But there are perils in such a course.

In 1990 Congress enacted a temporary phase-out of some itemized deductions (at the rate of 3 percent of the amount of adjusted gross income above $100,000 [indexed for inflation after 1991] but not to exceed 80 percent of those deductions). This was a devious way to increase the income tax rate without saying so, for a bracket varying in width with the amount of those itemized deductions for the taxpayer. Not only was it devious, but it is inconsistent with the premise that tax rates should increase as one's income increases. Once the phase-out of 80 percent of those itemized deductions is completed, the effective marginal tax rate drops, producing what some would call a "bubble." This phase-out of itemized deductions makes it difficult to say exactly what is the top marginal income tax rate—it is about 41 percent as a result of the phase-out alone. The 1993 Clinton Tax Bill made this phase-out of itemized deductions permanent. There also is a 2 percent phase-out of dependency deductions for those with incomes above certain levels. This also results in a bubble and increases the marginal rate above 41% percent for some persons.

One of the inequities of a progressive income tax is that two persons having the same total taxable income over a period of years, even though the income tax rates stay the same, can have substantially different total income tax liabilities. One with steady taxable income will pay much less income tax than another with fluctuating taxable income, averaging out to the same amount per year. Persons in small business and risk-takers are more likely to have fluctuating incomes. For instance, a homebuilder's income tends to fluctuate with mortgage interest rates. They pay this penalty inherent in a progressive income tax.

Through the years this was recognized as an injustice, and there were "averaging" provisions to mitigate the injustice. These provisions were complex. Under the Reagan-proposed 1986 Tax Reform Act, the averaging provision was repealed: it was complex and with lower rates the degree of injustice was more tolerable. With increasing tax rates, however, it is a significant injustice not to have an averaging provision.

The 1993 Clinton Tax Act enacted a provision denying any deduction for lobbying expenses, however relevant such expenses migh be to the taxpayer's business. This lobbying provision is an example of the superficiality and shallowness of the Treasury Department bureaucrats and Congressional staff who in 1993 were telling the Congressmen what to do in the income tax area. It is clear that proposed laws, regulations, and so on may have an adverse impact on various businesses and industries. For example, price controls on drugs and the pharmaceutical industry; or a huge excise tax increase on tobacco products and the various components of the tobacco industry. Surely, people in industry can express to their Congressmen and others their concerns about such proposals. Under a net income tax, the costs should be deductible.

There is a *de minimis* provision for in-house lobbying expenditures of less than $2,000. If $2,000 is exceeded, the entire lobbying expenditure is not to be deducted. For smaller businesses, my prediction is that the provision will be mostly ignored and that Internal Revenue will be able to do little about that noncompliance. But contempt for the Congress and the federal government will continue to grow among knowledgeable people.

The 1993 Clinton Tax Act reduced the percentage of business meals and entertainment expenses that are deductible from 80 percent to 50 percent. (This was discussed in Chapter 3 as an example of how the income tax is a controversy-generating machine.) When all the facts are known, some meals and entertainment expenses are clearly business expenses, some clearly are not, and others are arguable. There have been a series of provisions enacted over the years to impose stricter tests on the deductibility and the substantiation of these expenses. These have probably worked well for honest, conscientious taxpayers, but, since detailed audits of all businesses are impossible, probably have been ineffective overall. This Solomon-like 50 percent test can be justly criticized: it is a penalty on the business with such expenses which are clearly business-related, while it gives an undeserved break on such expenses which are clearly not business-related. The audit rate on such issues is likely to decline further, as agents see this as the solution to a vexing problem area.

One defect of our present income tax (which has eliminated the investment tax credit and lengthened the period for deductions to recover capital expenditures) is that a family developing a successful, capital intensive business is treated the same as one living solely on passive investments with a lavish, even wasteful, lifestyle. The Clinton high income tax rates unduly hurt pass-through business entities, such as partnerships and S corporations, which are capital intensive. These pay no federal income tax, but the income is reported by the owners and taxed to them. Relief is badly needed for these families, whose customers vote for them by buying their products. These families, who are growing the economy, are strained by paying the 39.6 percent (or higher) income tax rates while also coming up with funds to expand the business. Senator Roth (R-Delaware) has a bill introduced to give this relief. Combined with some investment tax credit and shorter depreciation lives, his bill could greatly assist a productive portion of our society.

Some of the provisions in the 1993 Clinton Tax Act are clearly troublesome, and merit review by the new Congress.

# 17
# A TAX ON ADJUSTED GROSS INCOME AS A SUBSTITUTE FOR THE PRESENT INCOME TAX

It is inherent in a net income tax that the cost of earning income (profits) be deducted in arriving at net income. However, a net income tax does not inherently require the deduction of consumption expenditures unrelated to any profit-seeking activity. Our current income tax law uses the term **adjusted gross income** which comes close to allowing the costs of earning income as deductions, but no consumption expenditures as deductions. The function served by adjusted gross income for individuals is that (apart from personal exemptions) they must waive the standard deduction to be able to itemize deductions in arriving at taxable income. Itemized deductions are almost all consumption expenditures, which Congress could, consistent with the spirit of a net income tax, not permit as deductions in arriving at taxable income.

A possible substitute for our present income tax would be an adjusted gross income tax. It would be simpler and would bring the resources of the Internal Revenue Service somewhat closer to those needed to achieve an adequate audit rate. An adjusted gross income tax would not permit deductions for some major categories of expenditures currently deductible, including property taxes on residences, interest on mortgage indebtedness on personal residences, charitable contributions, casualty losses on non business property, and medical expenses over a minimum amount.

Because the above deductions are taken by a large portion of the voting population who are generally articulate and influential, it probably would be a political impossibility to enact an adjusted gross income as a substitute for our present net income tax. The argument proponents of an adjusted gross income tax use is that eliminating these itemized deductions would broaden the base and permit a substantial reduction in rates for everyone, including those who now itemize. Another argument is that there is a discrimination under the present law against renters of housing and in favor of home owners. This is true. Home owners can deduct real property taxes and interest on their mortgage indebtedness. Renters cannot deduct any amount as a portion of the landlord's real property taxes and a portion of interest paid on any mortgage indebtedness by the landlord. This is true even though those costs are in almost all instances passed along to the renter as part of the rent paid.

Discriminations abound in our present income tax. To list and discuss them all would be impossible. The trend has been for Congress to add more discriminations. An adjusted gross income tax would be simpler than our present income tax. There are other supporting arguments which can be made for an adjusted gross income tax, but those who benefit from the existing itemized deductions probably have the political power to prevent eliminating all or even most of the existing itemized deductions.

Abolishing the income tax and replacing it with a national sales tax would avoid the issues of eliminating some deductions while keeping others.

# 18
# A GROSS INCOME TAX AS A SUBSTITUTE FOR OUR PRESENT NET INCOME TAX

Here is a one-sentence description of our federal net income tax: Gross income less deductions equals taxable income; taxable income times tax rate equals income tax liability. One suggestion for reducing the complexity of our present federal income tax is to eliminate all deductions and impose the tax upon gross income. With the base greatly broadened, the rates could be reduced to a small proportion of the current rates. Such a gross income tax would be much simpler than the present income tax.

There are problems with a gross income tax, however. A gross income tax would be contrary to the understanding of the state legislatures that ratified the sixteenth amendment; they contemplated a net income tax, that is, one on profits. The Supreme Court would have to decide if the gross income tax is constitutional.

But being stamped constitutional by the Supreme Court would not make a gross income tax sensible. Present law defines gross income from the sale of property as the price less the cost (the technical tax term is basis, which is more complicated than simple cost). If a gross income tax did not permit reduction of gross sales price by cost, it would be perceived as unfair. For instance, say a two-wage-earner couple buys a vacation home with only a small down payment and shortly afterward one wage earner becomes unemployed. By necessity, they sell the vacation home for about the purchase price, but as a result of the realtor's commission, they don't recover even their down payment. A gross tax on that total sales price would be an outrage, but one aspect of a gross income tax is that it is paid even when there is a loss.

A gross income tax would be grossly unfair to businesses and self-employed persons as compared to salaried persons and wage earners. Most salaried persons and wage earners have few, if any, expenses incurred in earning their salaries and wages. Their gross is almost all net. For a business with a net of only 1 percent of gross receipts the discrimination would be by a ratio of 100 to 1. For a business with a loss the discrimination might be called infinite or unmeasurable.

The basic cost of living,—food, clothes and shelter—would (I assume) not be deductible under a gross income tax, as under our present income tax. There probably would be personal exemptions and dependency deductions. As under present law, any personal exemptions might well be discriminatorily phased out for persons with higher gross incomes. This is a devious way to impose a higher tax rate without honestly calling it what it is.

These various fairness arguments against aspects of a gross income tax and the resultant political pressures probably would result in a gradual evolution of a gross income tax into a scheme having many of the complex characteristics of our present net income tax.

The economic dislocation from an immediate change from a net income tax to a gross income tax would be great, but difficult to predict. It would have a pyramiding effect on the price of goods moving through several taxpayers from original producer to consumer. For instance, wheat moves from farmer to grain elevator to flour miller to bakery to wholesaler to grocery store, with ancillary costs for transportation, state taxes, insurance, and so on. All these costs would be increased by the gross income tax paid by most providers. One of the arguments for a value added tax (VAT) is that it avoids this pyramiding effect of a gross income tax. But a VAT is complicated. It is discussed in chapter 21.

A gross income tax would not eliminate a major problem of our present tax system—massive cheating by those dealing in cash; however, a tax on consumption would cause those cheaters to increase their contributions toward Federal revenue.

# 19
# SUMMARY: WHY THE INCOME TAX SHOULD BE ABOLISHED

## The Reasons

1. A tax that costs the society and economy 65 percent of the revenue raised is intolerable.

2. Congress's record shows that an income tax can be a dangerous instrument in its hands: marriage penalty, percentage depletion, 1993 Clinton Tax Act, rules on charitable deferred giving, stock options, tax shelters, and capital gains (taxing illusory profits). Perhaps the worst was the 1986 transitional rules—tax indulgences were granted (sometimes probably sold) to permit some to escape the adverse consequences of the 1986 Tax Reform Act on many.

3. An income tax is unfair in a country with chronic inflation.

4. Complexity and other factors make fair treatment of all taxpayers under the income tax unachievable.

5. There are signs the income tax is breaking down: extensive cheating, the audit lottery, massive non-filing, tax protesters, an increasing backlog of uncollected assessments, and so on.

6. Discriminations exist under the income tax which cannot all be eliminated short of abolition of the income tax.

## The Process: What *You* Can Do

Achieving abolition of the income tax will require dedication. Absent some strong mitigating circumstance, vote against every Congressional incumbent who will not support abolition of the income tax. Write and tell your Congressmen that you plan to do so. Join organizations such as Citizens for an Alternative Tax System (1015 Oneonta Drive, Los Angeles, CA 90065), and the National Taxpayers Union (108 N. Alfred Street, Alexandria, VA 22314).

There will be opposition. There is an income tax industry with many persons engaged. The 65 percent direct and indirect costs—in addition to the income tax paid—resulting from our present federal tax system are putting lots of money in the pockets of many people.

Many tax attorneys and tax accountants will oppose abolition of the income tax. They shouldn't, for they know how awful the income tax is. But in a country short on intelligent, well-educated people, there will be many other opportunities for them. Tax accountants, freed of the burden of coping with an ever-changing, complicated income tax, can do more adequate work on conventional accounting. This will permit them to better assist managers of businesses in making decisions.

Some arguments in opposition have merit. For instance, the income tax can be said to favor charitable giving, but with the Reagan income tax cuts, charitable giving increased substantially. I.R.A.s combined with the income tax can be used to encourage saving; but abolition of the income tax and replacement with a national sales tax would increase savings much more. Retired persons living on savings from the funds left after the income tax should be granted relief from the national sales tax.

Those in the municipal bond industry and some in local and state government will oppose the abolition of the income tax (under which interest on municipal bonds is free from income tax). Abolition will end the ability of those governments to borrow at interest rates below market. Also, such bonds outstanding may drop in market value. But we must look to the overall good of the country. The loss to slaveowners didn't stop us from enacting the thirteentth amendment and freeing the slaves.

Abolition of the income tax will make the United States a tax haven for foreign capital. At present, in lieu of the income tax, there is a thirty (30) percent withholding tax on nonresident aliens on investment income, such as interest and dividends, from U.S. sources. There are statutory exceptions and this withholding has been modified by treaty with some countries. That withholding would cease entirely with the abolition of the income tax.

If Clinton is no longer president after January 20, 1997, the erosion of confidence abroad in our country should start reversing. With no income tax, capital from abroad will flow into the United States. Combined with increased domestic savings, increased available capital will cause interest rates to drop. Indeed, the price of municipal bonds may increase. This could occur because the interest rates on those bonds will be above the interest rates on newly issued federal and corporate bonds.

Some in the life insurance industry will want to cling to the income tax because the tax-free build-up of cash surrender value can be used to sell life insurance as a tax shelter from income taxation. But they are misguided. The unique nature of life insurance will cause that industry to get its share of increased savings after the abolition of the income tax.

Those who want to hold onto the income tax for some advantage they have under it are in effect asking to continue a discrimination in their favor.

## 20
## THE ARMEY FLAT TAX

A proposal by Congressman Dick Armey for a "flat tax" is currently getting attention in the news media. It is in part an adjusted gross income tax (discussed in chapter 17). Also Armey proposes deviation from major aspects of conventional accounting in determining the taxable income of business.

The Armey plan eliminates itemized deductions. Gone would be the deductions for interest on mortgage indebtedness on residences, property taxes on residences, state and local income taxes, and charitable contributions. Gone also would be the standard deduction.

Replacing the loss of these itemized deductions and the standard deduction would be these substantial annual allowances:

| | | |
|---|---|---|
| **1.** | **Single person** | **$13,100** |
| **2.** | **Head of Household** | **$17,200** |
| **3.** | **Married Couple** | **$26,200** |
| **4.** | **Each Dependent** | **$ 5,000** |

The marriage penalty would be gone, and the huge erosion in the real value of the dependency deduction from 1945 through 1994 would be corrected. These are great gains for the family. Not everyonewill gain, however. A person with a very large mortgage on a costly new residence would be a loser. One study, discussed in ***Fortune*** (June 12, 1995, p. 39) concluded that home values could drop by 15 percent and that mortgage interest rates might drop by a full percentage point as a result of the repeal of the home mortgage interest deduction. The home mortgage interest deduction is perceived as a major middle-class tax benefit.

The deduction for property taxes on the home also disappears under the Armey proposal. If realtors, home builders, and home mortgage lenders feel threatened, Congress will feel political pressure to reject these parts of the Armey proposal. The Nunn-Domenici USA Tax Proposal preserves the home mortgage interest deduction. Abolishing the income tax side steps these issues of what is to be deductible. A national sales tax replacing the income tax avoids this issue.

A major simplification for business under the Armey flat-tax plan is that it permits businesses to expense (deduct all at once) costs of capital equipment, structures, and land. This is a change from current law, under which the cost of equipment, machinery, and buildings is deducted over a period of time as depreciation. Land cost currently is not recovered until the land is sold or disposed of, with only the gain taxed as a capital gain.

The immediate deduction of capital costs would encourage investment and thus benefit the economy. If the Armey plan is enacted, a major issue will be what to do about the capital costs from prior years that have not yet been taken as depreciation deductions. Not to permit those ever to be deducted would be unfair under a net income tax (tax only the profit after deducting expenses of earning the profit). Permitting those depreciation deductions to continue combined with simultaneous deduction of new capital costs, however, would substantially reduce the revenue from the flat tax for several years. This would cause the rate to be higher for all taxpayers. The Armey plan calls for the same flat rate for both businesses and other taxpayers. Already some observers believe the flat rate projected by Armey is not high enough to replace the revenue from the current income tax.

Not only would the full cost of the capital expenditures be deducted currently, but also, under the Armey proposal, the full cost of goods purchased for resale would be deducted in the year of purchase. Inventories would not be used! The elimination of both depreciation accounting and inventory accounting would be a major simplification in the income tax. The Armey flat tax would be a substantial simplification of the present income tax, but would not replace it.

The Armey plan would permit a business to deduct the cost of merchandise bought late in the year, even though that merchandise would not be sold until the following year. This provides a tax planning opportunity to postpone payment of tax for one year by stocking up on inventory late in the year. Widespread postponement of tax payments might cause the revenue projections from the flat tax to be high, especially for the first few years it is in effect.

The news media have shown a post card on which wage earners and salaried persons can file their returns under the flat tax. But for business, the matter is more complicated. It is still a net income tax. The process of collecting all the gross income together and then deducting the business expenses, will require an "accounting." Whether on an IRS form or as an income statement prepared by an accountant, that process must occur. The income tax will be simplified by permitting the expensing of the cost of capital expenditures, thus eliminating depreciation, and also by not using inventories. But there will still be audits and disputes between the IRS and businesses. In fact, the simplification will enable revenue agents, who don't have to check depreciation and inventories, to audit other matters more closely.

One of the goals of the Armey flat tax is to avoid double taxation. An example of such double taxation is income taxed to corporations and then taxed again when distributed as dividends to stockholders. The Armey solution is to deny a deduction to the corporation so that a tax at the flat rate is paid by the corporation on the dividends. The dividend is not included in the income of the stockholder.

This solution will be divisive. Wage earners and salaried persons will be told that their wages and salaries are taxed, while the dividends of the "rich" are not taxed. The political fallout from this is likely to place the whole flat tax philosophy in jeopardy. With swings in the political pendulum, the flat tax, if enacted, may not be enduring.

A better solution would be to permit the corporation to deduct the dividend, thus avoiding a tax upon the corporation. The tax benefit of that deduction would improve the financial position of the corporation. This, in turn, would increase the market value of stocks. The dividend would be reported as income by the stockholder and taxed to the stockholder.

Interest paid by corporations is now deductible. The Armey flat tax proposal would deny a deduction to the corporation for interest paid. Also, like dividends, the interest received would be excluded from the income of the recipient. If the payee has no beneficial interest in the corporation, such as a bank or other financial institution, this will be very unpopular. This should be changed to permit the corporation to deduct the interest paid. The interest received would then be included in the income of the bond holder or the lender.

Under the current federal income tax, a business can deduct the cost of furnishing fringe benefits to its employees. Those employees do not have to report the fringe benefits as income. One of the largest fringe benefits is health insurance. This is discrimination against the self-employed and the employees of small businesses, who receive fewer fringe benefits than the employees of large businesses.

The Armey plan will not permit employers to deduct the cost of fringe benefits. Arguably, this is unfair, for the employer pays a tax on something the employees receive. But there would be administrative difficulties trying to tax employees on the value of all fringe benefits. You can't write a check to the IRS on your health insurance.

The Armey flat tax will not catch the cheaters who pay no income tax or much less than they should pay. A national sales tax, on the other hand, would tax everyone on his or her consumption expenditures. It should be recognized that abolishing the present income tax is the ultimate flat tax—zero. The Armey flat tax plan is in fact progressive. Until the much larger proposed, personal exemptions and dependency deductions are exhausted, the tax rate is zero. The overall effective tax rate then rises as the total income exceeds the personal exemptions and dependency deductions by larger amounts.

The flat tax, with much larger tax-free allowances and dependency deductions, would be a move back toward what the income tax was before World War II. That was before withholding, with which the income tax became a mass tax. Then only a small portion of individuals had to file income tax returns, and they wrote a single check when they filed their return. Almost half of American families would no longer pay income tax under the Armey plan, because of the more generous personal exemptions and dependency deductions. Withholding would be abolished, and taxpayers would pay income tax in monthly installments. This would make taxpayers aware of how much the government is costing them. [Ending withholding has been dropped from the Armey plan. The comments here are still relevant to this book and have not been deleted.]

How well would eliminating withholding work in practice? That remains to be seen. We do know from past experience that some employers, faced with other pressing cash needs, have failed to pay withheld tax on time. IRS collection officers have seized bank accounts of employers to pay these amounts (plus interest and horrendous penalties). This can put the employer out of business, leaving employees unemployed.

Under a flat tax with no withholding how will individuals fare who fail to make a monthly payment ? IRS is not a friendly creditor, and Congress has given IRS awesome collection powers. This is a potential problem area.

The sales tax is collected at the time of each sale by the seller. The taxpayer who makes the purchase thus has no chance to become delinquent and be pursued by IRS collection officers.The taxpayer will even have to file a return.

The Armey Flat Tax is still a net income tax, and under international agreements, this cannot be refunded on exports. Thus, under the Armey proposal, our businesses will still be at a competitive disadvantage in international trade. This would not be true of a sales tax. The sales tax would not apply to sales made outside the United States. So replacing the income tax with a national sales tax would improve our international competitiveness. Exports would increase and so would U.S. jobs. Foreign tourists also pay sales tax.

Payne's ***Costly Returns*** presents a compelling argument against the income tax. As noted, his study concluded that the total cost of the income tax in 1985 to the society and economy was 65 percent of the revenue received by the federal government. The flat tax would make only a partial reduction in those costs. Complete lifting of the huge and unproductive burden of the income tax would stimulate the economy. Abolition of the income tax would relieve citizens of a major source of controversy and animosity with their federal government.

Congress would be wise not merely to repeal the income tax, but also to submit a constitutional amendment repealing the sixteenthth amendment, and prohibiting a net income tax. Such an amendment might permit, in national emergencies, a gross income tax at a low rate, say, not to exceed 2 percent on businesses and 5 percent of investment income and compensation for services. Such a tax on investment income and compensation for services could be collected at the source by withholding. However, because of the poor record of Congress with the income tax, there should be a mechanism requiring approval by a majority of the states for imposition of any such gross income tax.

# 21
# NUNN - DOMENICI *USA* TAX PROPOSAL

A proposal by Senators Nunn and Domenici called the USA Tax Act of 1995 should receive serious consideration, if for no other reason than the fact the two senators proposing it are among the more respected members of the US Senate. It consists of two parts: First, it continues the individual income tax as a progressive tax on "consumed income." The key feature is an Unlimited Savings Allowance for individuals, which explains the name USA Tax. Second, it incorporates a value-added tax on all businesses (not just corporations), replacing the corporate income tax.

## The Consumed-Income Tax Portion

Senators Nunn and Domenici propose adding an unlimited savings allowance as a deduction in the individual income tax. This is in contrast to IRAs (Individual Retirement Accounts). IRAs are formal retirement accounts administered by some other person, such as a bank. Who can deduct is restricted, and an annual deduction is restricted to $2,000 a year. IRA plans are subject to various restrictions and penalties.

Deducting all the income saved each year, under the Nunn-Domenici proposal, means that an individual would only be taxed on what is consumed each year. The goal is to increase savings. This is a laudable goal. Our low savings rate combined with our budget deficit and trade deficit is a threat to our future, and possibly to the international financial structure.

Increased savings mean increased investment. Increased investment means economic growth, more employment, and higher standards of living. These, in the long run, mean more income tax collections for the government.

But Nunn-Domenici would be another step in the growth of complexity of the federal income tax. Individuals deduct what they reckon are their savings for the year (not total savings, but net, because withdrawal and spending of prior savings are income). The IRS currently audits largely from information returns of income reported by payers, with the social security number of the payee. This cannot be done for savings by individuals without some huge new reporting system.

Under Nunn-Domenici, income earned on savings would be tax exempt if saved and not spent. Capital gains would not be considered income as long as reinvested. But a withdrawal of either the original saved amount or of the income on savings which were also saved, would be reported as income and taxed. Savings before the USA tax becomes effective, which were from after-tax funds, could be withdrawn without being reported as income.

This unlimited savings allowance, if enacted as proposed, could become a large problem area. IRA accounts are handled by trained people, such as trust officers, and the annual additions are limited in amounts. Many individuals, based upon rumor and tips, would soon be claiming large, erroneous deductions as USA tax savings. Federal revenue could be much less than projected and the deficit would increase correspondingly.

To audit these unlimited savings allowances adequately would require a higher level of intrusiveness by revenue agents and an increase in the size of the IRS. The necessary training probably could not be done fast enough to avoid much confusion and disruption.

The USA tax bill purports to repeal the present individual income tax, but it actually re-enacts much of it by reference to section numbers or incorporation by reference. In short, it is not an abolition of the individual income tax.

There are many interesting concepts in the proposed USA Tax Bill for individuals:

1. A limited education expense deduction: $2,000 per family member per year to a maximum of $8,000;
2. A refundable credit for wage earners for Social Security taxes withheld from their pay (this would eliminate the regressivity of the Social Security tax);
3. Fringe benefits, including health insurance, to be income to employees;
4. Home mortgage interest deduction retained;
5. Charitable deduction retained;
6. The standard deduction is removed;
7. A recipient of a gift would include it in income to the extent spent;
8. The earned income tax credit increased, but eliminated if the wage earner has no children; and
9. It is a progressive tax with a maximum rate of 40 percent.

**Business Tax**

The USA tax repeals the corporate income tax and replaces it with a new tax on all businesses. Not merely corporations, but also sole proprietorships, partnerships, and any other non-corporate form of doing business are subject to this tax. It is proposed at a flat rate of 11 per- cent.

This would replace the corporate income tax. Since there are many complicated provisions in the corporate income tax, that would be a gain. While not called a value-added tax, it actually is. Such a tax would be less complicated then the existing corporate income tax, but still not simple. Since it has significant differences from an income tax, tax practitioners would have to work with both this new value-added tax as well as the progressive individual consumed income tax.

The starting point for this business tax is the gross receipts of the business. (This does not include financial receipts, such as interest and dividends.) Deducted are business purchases of property, rental of property, and services from another business. The businesses that furnish these to the purchasing businesses would have paid the value-added tax on those amounts. Note that this proposal does not require deducting the cost of capital expenditures over a period of time through depreciation. Instead, the full cost would be deducted in the year of expenditure. Also, inventory cost would be deducted when acquired rather than deducted in future years when sold through the use of inventories. Late in the year stocking up on inventory could be used to defer payment of this VAT until the next year.

Not deducted are wages and salaries paid to employees, cost of fringe benefits (unless included in the employee's income), retirement plan contributions, and interest paid on borrowed money. This is not a net income tax, as is the existing corporate income tax. The constitutional authority to levy this tax comes not from the sixteenth amendment but from the power to levy excise taxes, which was in the original Constitution.

The usual explanation of the value-added tax is that it is a consumption tax. Instead of being collected by the retail seller, it is collected by the various businesses handling the goods on the way to the hands of the ultimate consumer. There is a vast difference between a retail sales tax and a value-added tax. A retail sales tax is simple. It is collected on each transaction. Modern cash registers compute the sales tax, add it to the cost of the item sold, and record and add up sales tax totals (usually daily). The compliance cost to the retail merchant of a sales tax is small, almost trivial. Many businesses other than retailers will be involved with the value-added tax. The value- added tax is on a total amount, over a period of time rather than on each transaction. This involves recording much data and going through a "pulling together" process we call accounting. The value-added tax would be less complicated than the existing corporate net income tax, but it still would be complicated. The compliance costs would be less than with the corporate income tax, but not eliminated. Indeed, the compliance costs would be huge compared to a retail sales tax.

Compliance costs, of course, would ultimately be paid by the consumer. The compliance costs with the corporate income tax would begin gradually to disappear once the income tax returns for the last year subject to the corporate income tax are filed. Accounting and legal expenses from the corporate income tax would go on for years, as any professional involved in handling income tax controversies knows.

The European experience has been that value-added taxes inflate consumer prices. Abolishing the federal income tax and imposing a national retail sales tax simultaneously would be better for the consumer than Nunn-Domenici. Customers would have to pay the sales tax, but their income would not be reduced by withheld tax and declarations of estimated tax. So they would be in a good position to pay the sales tax.

Individuals would, as consumers, indirectly pay the value-added tax, plus some additional significant amount to cover compliance costs. They would also pay simultaneously the progressive, consumed-income tax under Nunn-Domenici.

## 22
## OTHER POSSIBLE PROPOSALS

On August 7, 1995 Secretary of the Treasury Rubin announced the Clinton Administration's support for the present income tax and its progressive rate structure. On August 28, 1995 a front page column in the Wall Street Journal revealed that the Clinton Administration was formulating and would announce a tax reform proposal.

The Rubin announcement, in effect, was a trial balloon, probably reflecting Clinton's real beliefs. Between August 7 and August 29 his pollsters convinced him that since the earlier position was a vote loser he should change his position. This is encouraging for it shows that the American people will support either an abolition of the income tax or a significant reduction of the evils of that tax by the enactment of a flat tax. There have been reports that the White House is interested in a value-added tax (Heritage Foundation, ***Backgrounder***, September 26, 1995, p.5).

Minority Leader Gephardt in the House of Representatives has announced what he calls a "10 Percent Tax." His stated goal is to obtain that rate for seventy-five percent of taxpayers, primarily employees. He would eliminate all itemized deducations except for interest on residential mortgages. The following table identifies the proposed tax rates, standard deductions and personal exemptions under his plan:

## 10% Tax

| Marginal Tax Rate | Married | Head of Household | Single |
|---|---|---|---|
| 10% | $0 - 40,200 | $0 - 32,250 | $0 - 24,050 |
| 20% | $40,200 - 97,150 | $32,250 - 83,250 | $24,050 - 58,300 |
| 26% | $ 97,150 - 148,150 | $ 83,250 - 134,850 | $ 58,300 - 121,600 |
| 32% | $148,150 - 264,450 | $134,850 - 264,150 | $121,600 - 264,150 |
| 34% | Income Over $264,450 | Income Over $264,450 | Income Over $264,450 |

## Standard Deduction

| | |
|---|---|
| Married | $8,350 |
| Head of Household | $7,350 |
| Single | $5,000 |

## Personal Exemption
## $2,750

The proposal contains nothing about the corporate income tax. The top twenty-eight percent rate on capital gains is to be repealed, so capital gains are taxed as ordinary income, including illusory gains caused by inflation. The anti-savings, anti-investment effect of the income tax will remain.

Gephardt's plan would tax fringe benefits (mainly health insurance) and employer pension contributions. For employees with the most generous health and retirement plans, the effective tax rate on available funds would approach 15 percent. He would tax the interest on municipal bonds, thus (if applied to existing bonds) the tax would operate as a capital levy by reducing the value of such bonds outstanding.

Since the marriage penalty and the complexity and compliance costs for businesses, both small and large, would remain, this proposal, unless changed substantially, does not merit serious consideration.

# 23
# A NATIONAL SALES TAX

We need to flee from the complex, controversy-generating income tax to a simple tax. The sales tax is a simple, broad-based tax. It is computed transaction by transaction, not on a combined accounting for all transactions over a period of time. Modern cash registers compute sales tax on each transaction and total the tax over a period of time, such as a day. This means the cost to the retail merchant is minimal. Everyone pays it, and it is progressive, because the rich spend more than the poor. The sales tax is simple enough that the news media should be able to explain new legislation so the public can understand and take appropriate action at the ballot box.

The income tax takes away from businesses and investors funds that could be spent by them more productively than by the government. Further, it imposes huge compliance costs on the private sector. Abolition of the income tax would lead to even greater economic performance than that following the 1981 Reagan tax cut.

The market values of stock are largely based on after-income tax earnings. Abolition of the income tax would increase enormously the total market value of stocks. "Professor Dale Jorgensen of Harvard estimates that national wealth would immediately rise by a trillion dollars if a flat rate consumption tax is implemented," says Bartlett in his article "Will the Flat Tax KO Housing?," ***Wall Street Journal***, (August 2, 1995, p. A10). Those increases in the value of stocks would increase the net worth of individual stockholders, pension funds holding stock (and thus increase the security of pension recipients both current and future), endowment funds of non-profit organizations, and others. This increase in net worths would be conducive to new ventures in the private sector, the real source of wealth in our economy.

We would replace a tax on investment, with one on consumption.

At present, U.S. citizens have a meager savings rate and largely rely on foreign sources to fund budget deficits and trade deficits. Savers face two taxes: one on the income saved, and another on the interest, dividends, or other income received on the savings. Abolishing the income tax would increase savings and increased savings may be our salvation by helping avoid the disaster that will ultimately come from the combination of budget deficits, trade deficits, and meager savings.

The host of people who are cheating on the income tax or winning at playing the audit lottery, would pay the sales tax on their consumption.

A study done by John H. Qualls at Washington University in St. Louis concluded that a national sales tax at a rate of 17 percent could replace the revenue presently raised by the income tax. That may sound high, but remember incomes go up immediately through elimination of withholding and payment of estimated tax. Here is a summary of the Qualls study:

> The replacement of the current U.S. individual and corporate income taxes by a national sales tax would result in faster economic growth, higher levels of employment, more business investment, higher productivity growth, and an increase in the private savings rate.
>
> These results were obtained from an econometric simulation using a variation of the Washington University Macroeconomic Model (WUMM), available commercially from Laurence H. Meyer and Associates

(LHM&A), a St. Louis-based economic consulting and forecasting firm.

A one-for-one replacement of the personal and corporate income taxes with a national sales tax results in a reallocation of GNP away from consumption and toward investment. The investment share of GNP rises two percentage points (from 17.1 percent to 19.1 percent) with the introduction of a national sales tax.

The private savings rate (total of personal and business savings) rises from 15.4 percent up to 18.1 percent after the introduction of a national sales tax.

Real business investment is from 19 to 25 percent higher with a national sales tax. In effect, businesses use the extra cash flow resulting from the elimination of the income tax to invest in plant and equipment.

The higher level of capital stock results in more employment. The number of new jobs generated by the national sales tax reaches 900,000 by 2000 and 1,600,000 by the year 2010.

Because of the increase in business investment, real GNP grows at a faster rate after introduction of a national sales tax. Although the annual growth rate differential seems small, at 0.2 percent it results in a significantly higher level of real GNP by the year 2010 — up 4.1 percent. This amounts to a difference of over $1,500 (in constant 1990 dollars) for every person of working age in the country, or over $3,100 for a family with two working-age adults.

The national sales tax is not inflationary. Although the price of goods (including the tax) would reflect a one-time price increase, the rate of increase in prices after that would actually be lower by 0.2 percent per year. Thus, sustained inflation would drop after introduction of the sales tax and abolishment of the income tax.

> In short, implementation of a national sales tax would go a long way toward rectifying the U.S.'s decline in international competitiveness.

A study by Laurence J. Kotlikoff, professor of economics at Boston University corroborates the conlcusions of the Qualls study. This study, entitled ***The Economic Impact of Replacing Federal Income Taxes with a National Sales Tax***, was sponsored by the Cato Institute and released in 1993. It concludes that the abolition of the federal income tax and replacement with a national sales tax would increase savings and hence available capital, and increase wages in real terms.

For businesses, cash flow would increase from the disappearance of federal income tax payments and the end of the huge, unproductive cost of income tax compliance. The added available cash would make funds available for increased investment in plant, equipment, and working capital.

The federal income tax is a cost that must be recovered through sales prices high enough to achieve an adequate profit margin. Abolition of the federal income tax should (through the competitive process) decrease prices to consumers, tending to offset the national sales tax addition to the cost of retail purchases (also offset for the consumer by the end of withholding of income tax and the payment of estimated income tax).

Such a plan would be a strong motivation for U.S. corporations not to locate plants in foreign countries, which impose an income tax on US corporations doing business in their countries. Also, export prices could be decreased to reflect the abolition of the federal income tax and the resultant elimination of the huge costs of compliance. The resultant improvement in our international competitive position should decrease our trade deficit and perhaps even eliminate it.

For individuals, the end of income tax withholding and payment of estimated tax would occur simultaneously with the imposition of the national sales tax. But the motivation for savings would be substantially increased, because the saver would no longer have the income on savings reduced by the federal income tax. To avoid the sales tax being a burden on low-income persons, there should be a refund of standard amounts of sales tax to such persons and to retird persons living on savings on which income tax has been paid. There would need to be strict safeguards, of course.. Don't forget that the IRS has made "refunds" to prison inmates based upon phony withholding forms. There is also fraud involving the earned income credit—for example, reporting non-existent earnings to get the refund. The working poor on their own mostly do not understand this refundable credit and don't claim it. Sharpies claim it for them, and probably get much of the refunds, which they don't report as income.

Excise taxes could be used to satisfy the widespread desire to "do something" to people who "have too much money." For instance, an excise tax on advertising on the broadcast or telecast of professional sports could reduce the excessive salaries there. Excise taxes could also be used to inhibit the officers of publicly owned corporations from getting excessive compensation, thereby breaching their fiduciary duty to the stockholders. An annual license tax to smoke could ultimately reduce enormously the medical costs paid by the federal and state governments.

While the top rates under the estate and gift tax should be reduced, and relief should be given for family businesses that stay in the family, estate and gift taxes will remain.

## CONCLUSION

In recent years the growth rate of the United States economy has fallen below the historic pattern. Real wages in recent years have been stagnant—dollar increases in wages merely offset the increase in the cost of living. Budget deficits, continued growth of the national debt, and persistent huge trade deficits are warning signals. The income tax, that is anti-savings and anti-investment, and that adversely affects our international competitiveness must be abolished. Burdensome government regulations join the income tax as a cause of our problems.

The best choice to replace the income tax is a national sales tax. This will increase savings, investment, and employment. A flat tax will be a significant improvement, but it still is a net income tax. Audits will continue. A Net income tax is inherently complicated, and Congress—urged by the Treasury Department—has added mind-boggling complexity. This tax generates much controversy between citizens and government.

Increased economic growth and elimination of the trade deficit will follow abolition of the income tax and a rational reduction of burdensome government reglations. Without increased economic growth, other problems such as the decline in the quality of education and increased crime will not be solved.

## TOPICAL INDEX